HELEN DIXON

CW00959450

Welcome...

"Millions of photographers around the world are passionate about capturing beautiful landscapes. This shouldn't come as a surprise, as there are few feelings that can beat returning home from a long day's photography with memory cards filled with stunning scenes. But it is a form of photography that presents you with many challenges. You need to be prepared for long hours, with early starts to reach a location before sunrise and picture-taking often continuing until after sunset. And you'll also have to brave all sorts of weather conditions in your quest to capture a glorious scene. All the trials and tribulations you've endured are quickly forgotten, though, when you discover what stunning images you've captured. *The Essential Guide to Landscape Photography* is packed with photo technique, expert guides and stunning photography and aims to deliver all the information, advice and inspiration you need to improve your photo skills. It's brimming with tutorials from many of the UK's most popular outdoor photographers, with emphasis on key in-camera techniques, as well as essential and creative post-processing skills. We hope it helps you take your best ever landscape images. All the best!"

DANIEL LEZANO, EDITOR

Meet our landscape experts

All our experts are regular contributors to *Digital SLR Photography* magazine. For expert advice and inspiration to help you improve your photo skills, pick up the latest issue, available on the second Tuesday of every month. For further information, visit: www.digitalslrphoto.com

ROSS HODDINOTT
Ross is an award-winning photographer with many years of experience capturing the diverse beauty of Britain's landscapes and wildlife.
www.rosshoddinott.co.uk

HELEN DIXON
Helen is living the dream, having given up a full-time job to become a professional landscape photographer. She is one of the UK's brightest talents.
www.helendixonphotography.co.uk

LEE FROST
A pro for two decades, Lee Frost's one of the best-known names in the UK photography business, with 20 books to his name and worldwide image sales.
www.leefrost.co.uk

ADAM BURTON
A highly successful landscape photographer with an extensive portfolio of images, Adam is the author of the photography book *The Dorset Coast*.
www.adam-burton.co.uk

The Essential Guide to Landscape Photography

Produced by *Digital SLR Photography* at:
6 Swan Court, Cygnet Park,
Peterborough, Cambs PE7 8GX
Phone: 01733 567401. Fax 01733 352650
Email: enquiries@digitalslrphoto.com
Online: www.digitalslrphoto.com

Editorial
To contact editorial phone: 01733 567401
Editor **Daniel Lezano**
daniel_lezano@dennis.co.uk
Art Editor **Luke Marsh**
luke_marsh@dennis.co.uk
Features Editor **Caroline Wilkinson**
caroline_wilkinson@dennis.co.uk
Features Writer **Jordan Butters**
jordan_butters@dennis.co.uk
Designer **Luke Medler**
luke_medler@dennis.co.uk
Editorial Co-ordinator **Jo Lezano**
jo_lezano@dennis.co.uk

Editorial contributors:
Ross Armstrong, Mark Bauer, Adam Burton,
Helen Dixon, Lee Frost, Ross Hoddinott & John Patrick

Advertising & Production
Display & Classifield Sales: 020 7907 6651
Advertising Sales **Guy Scott-Wilson**
guy_scott-wilson@dennis.co.uk
Sales Executive **Joshua Rouse**
joshua_rouse@dennis.co.uk
Production Controller **Daniel Stark**
daniel_stark@dennis.co.uk
Digital Production Manager **Nicky Baker**
nicky_baker@dennis.co.uk

Management
MAGBOOK PUBLISHER **DHARMESH MISTRY**
OPERATIONS DIRECTOR **ROBIN RYAN**
MD OF ADVERTISING **JULIAN LLOYD-EVANS**
NEWSTRADE DIRECTOR **DAVID BARKER**
COMMERCIAL & RETAIL DIRECTOR **MARTIN BELSON**
PUBLISHING DIRECTOR **JOHN GAREWAL**
CHIEF OPERATING OFFICER **BRETT REYNOLDS**
GROUP FINANCE DIRECTOR **IAN LEGGETT**
CHIEF EXECUTIVE **JAMES TYE**
CHAIRMAN **FELIX DENNIS**

CONTENTS

7 Introduction to landscapes
Be prepared to learn and exploit the
fundamentals of landscape photography

8 Composition
The key techniques you'll want to master to
take perfect landscapes, including lead-in lines,
foreground interest and natural frames

21 Exposure
Master these simple techniques and you'll be
on your way to well-exposed landscapes
22 EXPERT TUTORIAL: APERTURE-PRIORITY
24 EXPERT TUTORIAL: SHUTTER SPEEDS
26 EXPERT TUTORIAL: MAXIMISING DETAIL

30 Lighting
Learn how to make the most of any lighting
condition, from sunrise through to sunset
36 EXPERT ADVICE: TIME OF DAY
38 EXPERT ADVICE: MAGIC HOUR & SUNSETS
40 EXPERT ADVICE: WEATHER

43 Sharpness
The best techniques for super-sharp scenics
44 EXPERT TUTORIAL: HYPERFOCAL FOCUSING
46 EXPERT TUTORIAL: FOCUS FOR SHARPNESS

48 Raw & landscapes
Maximise image quality by shooting in Raw
52 EXPERT ADVICE: UNDERSTANDING ACR
54 EXPERT TUTORIAL: PROCESSING RAW FILES
56 EXPERT TUTORIAL: MERGING RAW FILES
58 EXPERT TUTORIAL: EXPOSING TO THE RIGHT

60 Filters
Use filters to improve and enhance your shots
62 EXPERT ADVICE: USING AN ND GRAD
64 EXPERT ADVICE: USING A POLARISER
66 EXPERT ADVICE: USING AN ND FILTER
68 EXPERT ADVICE: THE TEN-STOP ND FILTER
70 EXPERT TUTORIAL: USING AN ND GRAD

72 Water in landscapes
Why water works so well in landscapes
78 EXPERT TUTORIAL: SHOOT NATURAL WAVES
80 EXPERT TUTORIAL: BLURRING MOTION
82 EXPERT TUTORIAL: SHOOT RUNNING WATER
84 EXPERT TUTORIAL: FRAMING A LIGHTHOUSE

87 Colour and black & white
Learn the relationship of colour in scenes
88 EXPERT ADVICE: COLOUR THEORY
90 EXPERT ADVICE: COLOUR & WHITE BALANCE
94 PHOTOSHOP TUTORIAL: B&W CONVERSION

97 Expert Gems: Seasons
Brilliant ideas to keep you busy all year round

107 Landscape projects
Fantastic techniques leading to stunning scenics
108 EXPERT TUTORIAL: SHOOT PANORAMICS
110 EXPERT TUTORIAL: BEAUTY OF BLUEBELLS
112 EXPERT TUTORIAL: MISTY MORNINGS
114 EXPERT TUTORIAL: COASTAL SCENES
116 EXPERT TUTORIAL: SCENIC SILHOUETTES
118 EXPERT TUTORIAL: STAR TRAILS
120 EXPERT TUTORIAL: MOONLIT LANDSCAPES

123 Photoshop techniques
Simple Photoshop step-by-steps that can be used
to improve and enhance your landscape images
124 PHOTOSHOP TUTORIAL: BOOST DULL SCENES
126 PHOTOSHOP TUTORIAL: ADD A GRAD FILTER
128 PHOTOSHOP TUTORIAL: ADD MIST & MOOD
130 PHOTOSHOP TUTORIAL: REPLACE A SKY
132 PHOTOSHOP TUTORIAL: SEASONAL BLUR
134 PHOTOSHOP TUTORIAL: ADD AN ND EFFECT
136 PHOTOSHOP TUTORIAL: ADD MONO DRAMA
138 PHOTOSHOP TUTORIAL: MONO INFRARED

140 Landscape gear
The best equipment for outdoor photography
141 IDEAL KITS FOR _YOUR_ REQUIREMENTS
146 WIDE-ANGLE LENSES
148 EXPERT TUTORIAL: WIDE-ANGLE LENSES
150 BEST BUYS: WIDE-ANGLE LENSES
152 EXPERT TUTORIAL: TELEZOOMS
154 FILTER SYSTEMS
158 CHOOSING THE RIGHT TRIPOD
160 CHOOSING THE RIGHT BAG

162 Perfect exposures
Cut out and use our free grey card!

TURN TO PAGE 122 TO FIND OUT ABOUT
OUR FANTASTIC SUBSCRIPTION OFFERS

The big-lens outdoor backpack

We've expanded our award-winning Flipside series with a large-capacity backpack that offers maximum protection and organization for pro-level gear. It has a really large main compartment that includes space for a 500mm lens—yet it's amazingly lightweight and weighs 4.3 pounds before you pack it. If you're looking for all-day comfort and quick access to valuable gear, the **Flipside 500 AW** is your comfortable solution for the great outdoors.

Find your perfect bag at **Lowepro.com** or call **0845 250 0792.** You can also follow us on  @LoweproUK

Lowepro®

The **Trusted Original**™ Since 1967

THE BASICS

CAPTURE STUNNING LANDSCAPES – we all want to be able to do it. Fantastic landscapes inspire more photographers than any other type of image and on the face of it, well, it should be easy to do. Find an awesome vista and point your camera at it, press the shutter and that should do the trick. This simple approach will probably bag you a decent snap, but often the image you capture will not do justice to the glorious scene in front of you. We've all been a little bit disappointed by a photo that doesn't quite live up to our great expectations. The difference between a decent snap and a stunning image is often down to a few versatile ideas, some easily-learned expert knowledge, the right equipment choice and careful planning. This inspirational guide will provide you with an excellent grasp of these fundamentals and help you transform your shots from the ordinary into something very special indeed.

REVISED & UPDATED
TECHNIQUE & ADVICE FROM THE EXPERTS!

ADAM BURTON

COMPOSITION

MORE THAN ANY OTHER factor, composition can turn an okay image into a masterpiece. There are a small number of techniques that, once learned, will serve you well in many different situations.

Composing the elements in the frame is a skill of taking great pictures. Carefully consider how points of interest are arranged and how they relate to each other.

Placing a subject centrally in the frame usually results in a static rather than dynamic composition. Placing the subject off-centre, encourages the eye to move around the frame more. One way of dividing the frame up to achieve harmony is to use the rule-of-thirds (see below). This proportion often occurs in nature, and there is research to suggest that our brains are hard-wired to find these arrangements more attractive.

1) The rule-of-thirds

This is a simple way of organising the elements in the frame so that they create a balanced composition. As a compositional tool, it's been around for a few centuries and is a simplified version of the 'golden section', which is used in art and architecture.

Imagine two vertical lines dividing the viewfinder into thirds. Now do the same with two horizontal lines. You then organise the main elements of the picture within this grid. For example, with a simple landscape, place the horizon on one of the lines, so that you have two-thirds land and one third sky, or vice-versa.

If you have a strong focal point, such as a tree or building, you can place it on one of the points where the horizontal and vertical lines intersect. This will make a much more dynamic composition than if you were to place the focal point centrally, which can make a picture look rather static. Inexperienced photographers often put the subject right in the middle and it rarely works.

Moving an element of a scene to a different intersection can create a startlingly different image, such is the power of the rule-of-thirds. Don't be afraid to experiment with different variations on a theme.

RULE-OF-THIRDS GRID: This image follows the rule-of-thirds quite closely. There is approximately two-thirds land/sea and one-third sky. The lighthouse and obelisk are divided by the left vertical, each equal distant from it.

2) Foreground interest

The problem is that the world is three-dimensional but a photograph is two-dimensional, so one of the main reasons that landscape images fail is that they don't convey the sense of depth that our eyes see. Fortunately, there are a few compositional tricks that we can employ to get around this rather frustrating little problem.

A very effective way to create depth in a photograph is to include a strong foreground, often in conjunction with a wide-angle lens. Emphasising the foreground in this way will add depth to the picture by creating an entry-point for the eye, pulling the viewer into the scene and giving the picture a sense of distance and scale.

Wide-angle lenses help this technique because they stretch perspective, exaggerating the elements close to the lens and opening up the view beyond the foreground.

But be careful, this can result in the middle distance looking empty and lacking in interest so the trick is to shoot from a lower viewpoint. This compresses the middle distance, so that there isn't too much empty space in the composition. You'll also need to use a small aperture and focus carefully to maximise depth-of-field, keeping foreground and distant objects in focus (we'll explain how to do this later).

GETTING IT RIGHT: The cow parsley and gorse make attractive foregrounds to lead the eye into the scene and provide suitable frames for the view beyond. A wide-angle lens and a small aperture of f/22 provide plenty of depth-of-field.

BIG FOREGROUND OR SMALL DETAIL: It's not always necessary to have a large foreground; colour, texture and pattern can provide attractive foreground interest. The carpet of flowers is as effective as the strong shapes of rocks, opposite.

3) Lead-in lines

Lines represent depth in a picture and can be used to lead your eye into the picture and guide it around the scene.

Lines are everywhere: man-made, such as roads, paths and hedgerows, or natural, such as rivers or the coastline – all will add dynamism to your photographs. Lines don't have to be real, they can be 'implied' like the patterns created by waves over a longish exposure, or objects pointing into the frame. Lots of things can bring linear energy into your work.

Straight, converging lines are very dynamic and can give a lot of impact to a picture, but there is always the danger that the eye follows the lines into and then very quickly out of the frame again. Pictures with only converging lines might have immediate impact, but can still be unsatisfying. It's a good idea to try and place some object of interest within the frame – a figure or a tree, for example – to give the eye something to settle on within the scene.

Lines that curve gently in an 'S' shape lack the immediate impact of straight, converging lines, but can result in a more satisfying image. They can lead the eye gently through the whole picture, allowing the viewer to take in other elements within the composition.

4) Layers and planes

Another in-camera technique that can be used to add depth to an image is the creation of a layered effect. Layers in an image can be created by having a series of overlapping shapes (see right) or by strong side-lighting, creating alternative bands of light and shade that can give the effect of a layering of light.

This kind of technique works particularly well with longer lenses that compress perspective and stack overlapping forms. Each layer, or plane, appears thinner and closer to the next, exaggerating the effect. Just remember longer lenses will produce less depth-of-field so you'll need to use smaller apertures, such as f/16, if elements are in the foreground or near middle distance.

This shot was taken at dawn near Lyme Regis using a 70-200mm zoom at around 100mm. The longer focal length compresses the distances between the layers and the strong, directional light helps emphasise the layers – the early morning mist add bags of atmosphere.

Keep it simple!
Composition is all about what you choose to include in the frame – and also what you choose to leave out. Often, less is more and compositions that are uncluttered can be the most successful

5) Break the rules!

Like all rules, the rule-of-thirds needs to be applied with judgement rather than as a matter of course and there will always be situations where it can be ignored. For example, when shooting a scene where the sky is reflected in water, you might want to place the horizon across the middle of the frame, giving the two elements of the shot – sky and reflection – equal weighting.

If there is no interest in the sky, place the horizon higher in the frame or crop it out altogether. To increase a sense of emptiness and isolation, the horizon can be placed very low in the frame. The beauty of shooting digitally is the ease at which you can review your efforts and experiment to ensure the perfect composition.

6) Find natural frames

A popular compositional device is to use something to frame the view beyond, such as an archway, doorway, window or the overhanging branches of trees.

Try using frost-covered plants and gateposts to create a natural frame for the main subject of your shot. Use the frame to lead the viewer's eye into the scene for some truly eye-catching results.

Control your focus and depth-of-field carefully though. While a small aperture often works best, blurring the frame significantly can help keep attention on the main subject. If you do want to render your frame out of focus, make sure you blur it enough so that the effect looks deliberate and not like a mistake in focusing.

7) Experiment with viewpoints

Finding the right viewpoint is key to successful landscape composition. Rather than shooting everything from head height, experiment with high and low viewpoints.

Higher viewpoints have the effect of opening up the planes in the image and is useful with standard and telephoto lenses. When photographing well-known landmarks, it's tempting to use the established viewpoints, but spend time looking for a fresh view, as it's much more satisfying to capture something original.

While there's nothing wrong with the first picture, it's the 'standard' view of Old Harry Rocks in Dorset. Without having to move very far, however, a less photographed and more dramatic viewpoint has been found.

Lead-in lines

Master the first of three crucial compositional tools: lead-in lines

FEW COMPOSITIONAL devices can improve the impact and add depth to your landscape pictures as well as lead-in lines. While we've touched on the basics, we think it deserves a little more consideration.

When you think of lead-in lines, what comes to mind? Rows of crops, a seemingly never-ending road, a bendy stream? What about shadows, footprints, clouds, the coastline, windows, piers, cracks, paths or rocks – the list can go on and on. Although lead-in lines come in many guises, some natural, others man-made, all of them tend to either lead the viewer in and out of the picture or towards a focal point. The latter being the preferred choice as it allows the eye to settle within the scene, but both can work well depending on the picture.

Some of the most effective lead-in lines start from the bottom edge of the frame and go straight in to the centre of the picture, like a pier towards the horizon, but there are many variations that can have just as much impact, depending on the scene. While straight lines quickly draw the eye to the point of interest, curved lines force the viewer to take a more leisurely journey through the image. Vertical lines, shot from a low angle, like those on a building, add tension to a picture and diagonal lines work well if they travel from the bottom left to the top right of a picture, as that's where the human eye naturally gravitates. It doesn't have to be a single line either: multiple lines only strengthen the effect of one line, as long as they're clearly defined and heading in the same direction. It's important to keep the elements in a scene connected, as any break

in the flow of the line will leave the composition feeling disjointed and the viewer's gaze to wander aimlessly.

You can enhance your lead-in lines depending on what viewpoint and lens you choose, as both can either flatten or stretch perspective. The most dynamic distortion of lead-in lines is converging verticals. Converging diagonal lines create a powerful impression of distance and depth, especially if they converge in to the centre of the frame and run parallel to each other. By standing in the middle of them you'll find that the further the lines are away from the camera, the closer they get to each other, creating what's known as a vanishing point when they join. A wide-angle lens can greatly enhance this effect as it stretches perspective so the lines seem wider at the start and narrower in the distance, whereas a telephoto lens compresses perspective and hinders the feeling of depth.

1) Lead-in lines don't have to be straight or lead to a focal point: the line can also be the interest in the picture. Note how your eye is led through the scene by the wintry tree-lined road.

2) When using converging verticals, you need to get the entire scene in focus. Set the camera on a tripod and select a small aperture (f/11 – f/22) and focus on the hyperfocal distance for maximum depth-of-field.

3) Simple compositions can sometimes be the most effective. Think about creating a graphic coastal landscape with nothing more than groynes or a pier as a lead-in line. By connecting it to the horizon too, it means the viewer's gaze is led in to the far reaches of the scene and led out of the frame by the horizon line.

4) Diagonal lines can be used to draw the gaze from bottom left to top right, where the eye naturally gravitates, as in this coastal landscape, where the lines of rocks converge towards the stunning sunset sky.

5) The fence in this picture is used as a neat device to draw the eye in towards the focal point, the elevated castle in the distance.

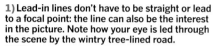

Lead-in lines: Think differently

Try photographing lead-in lines from different angles. You may find that photographing the lines entering the frame at an angle work better than if you captured them starting within in the frame. The opposite can be true, too. Try different perspectives: get low to the ground for extreme converging verticals. Tilt the camera up to see what vertical lines you can find and try to elevate your position by standing on a bridge, for instance. Above all, keep your eyes and your mind open for less obvious linear aspects and don't forget the other guidelines for composition, including foreground interest and the rule-of-thirds.

Shadows   Texture   Footprints

Foreground interest

A few compositional tricks will improve your photography no end: swot up on foreground interest to give your shots depth and scale

THE LATE, GREAT war photographer Robert Capa once said, "If a picture's not good enough, you weren't close enough." He was talking about capturing the drama of human conflict, of course, and the need to be in the heart of the action – an approach that unfortunately eventually cost him his life. However, the same maxim can easily be applied to landscape photography because if you want to capture the drama of a great scene, you need to move in close and make the most of the foreground – it's one of the important elements you need to create a dynamic composition.

Foreground interest is useful for a number of reasons. First and foremost, emphasising the foreground will help to give your photographs a sense of distance and scale. This is due to perspective – features close to the camera look much bigger than those further way, so our brain immediately registers that the smaller features must be in the distance and we see the image as three-dimensional, making it more realistic.

Secondly, the foreground provides a convenient entry point into the composition for the viewer's eye, which then naturally travels up through the scene to the focal point or the background. A successful composition needs a 'hook' to entice the viewer and hold the attention. With landscapes, the foreground is that hook.

Thirdly, the foreground contains more information than the rest of the scene, and being closest to the camera allows you to record fine detail that isn't affected by haze, mist and fog like features that are more distant.

Wide-angle lenses are the most useful for exploiting foreground interest as they allow you to include elements in a shot that are literally at your feet. The way wide-angle lenses 'stretch' perspective also makes those elements loom large in the frame while everything else seems to rush away into the distance. The lower the viewpoint you adopt, the more the foreground will dominate.

Lenses with a focal length of 16-18mm (24-28mm on full-frame sensors) are a relatively safe bet to begin with as they're wide enough to include lots of foreground interest without being so wide that you end up with all foreground and nothing else. Once your confidence grows you can produce amazing images with super-wide lenses from 10-15mm (15-22mm full-frame), but you need to get really close to the foreground otherwise it will seem miles away due to the excessive 'stretching' of perspective you get with these wider lenses.

Telephoto lenses are less dynamic in this respect as the foreground interest you include is formed by elements or features in the scene that are obviously further away, while the foreshortening or perspective 'squeezes' the elements together so you don't get the same sense of distance and three dimensions. Nevertheless, the effect can still be strong, with a single feature dominating the foreground.

What can be used as foreground interest? Pretty much anything – rocks, rivers, walls, gates, fences, trees, moored boats, sand ripples, reflections, people. Features and elements in the scene that create natural or assumed lines work the best of all as they lead the viewer's eye into and through the scene. Lines that travel vertically work well, lines that travel diagonally from bottom left to top right work even better, and lines that converge into the distance, such as railway tracks or straight roads, are the most powerful of all. To make the most of vertical and converging lines, turn your camera on its side and shoot in portrait format. Diagonal lines are better shot in landscape format as they have further to travel through the composition, holding attention for longer.

1) Use a wide-angle lens to 'stretch' perspective and a low viewpoint to make the foreground interest more prominent.

2) Try picking subjects that form diagonal lines that lead from the bottom left to the top right of the frame, like these boats do, as it draws the viewer in to the picture.

3) Instead of using foreground interest as a prelude to a distant focal point, try composing pictures where the dominant subject is in the foreground and keep the background simple.

4) One good reason why you shouldn't leave home without an array of ND grad filters is to ensure your foreground is correctly exposed. In low-light conditions, like a sunset, it's easy to render the foreground dark and distracting.

5) Practically anything can work as foreground interest, as long as it's composed well and fits with the rest of the scene. Look for unusual subjects or for objects that you may never have considered using before, such as driftwood, shells or wreckage remains.

6) Rocks are the most popular subjects to use in a coastal landscape and can be the most effective when used as a lead-in line, also. Jetties and piers work well too and have the added bonus of you being able to introduce converging verticals.

Maximise depth-of-field

There's no point including fantastic foreground if it's out of focus; what you need is enough depth-of-field for front-to-back sharpness. As a rule of thumb, if you use a camera with an APS-C sensor with a focal length around 16-18mm, focus the lens on a point 1.5m from the camera, stop down to f/11 and everything will be sharp from around 75cm to infinity. For wider focal lengths in the 10-15mm range, focus on a point one meter away, stop down to f/11 and everything will be sharp from around 50cm to infinity. For full-frame DSLRs with a focal length in the 24-28mm range, focus on a point 1.5m away, stop down to f/16 and depth-of-field will extend from around 75cm to infinity. For wider lenses in the 16-20mm range, focus on 1m, stop down to f/16 and you'll get depth-of-field from around 50cm to infinity. Basically, to maximise depth-of-field with wide-angle lenses, you need to focus on a point relatively close to the camera; many photographers focus further into the scene, resulting in an unsharp image.

How to use natural frames

For ideas, inspiration and information on how to improve your landscape pictures with environmental frames, read on...

ONE OF THE MOST effective ways of producing a tight, structured composition is by framing the scene or subject you're shooting. Not only does this help to direct the viewer's eye towards the most important part of the picture, but frames can also be used to hide uninteresting areas, such as a broad expanse of empty sky. Natural frames can be used in all types of photography but are abound in the landscape if you keep your eyes peeled.

When you think of natural frames, what comes to mind? The overhanging branches of a tree are perhaps the most obvious. The gap between trees that frames the scene beyond? How about overhanging cliffs or the entrance to a cave? On the coast, the gaps between rock outcrops or cliffs can be used to frame the beach and sea beyond.

These are all fairly obvious options, but if you start to think laterally other ideas will present themselves. For example, the shape of a hillside or mountain can be used to frame features positioned in front of it. Clouds in the sky can act like a frame, too – containing elements on the ground and forcing the eye down towards them.

When shooting using a frame and the sun is behind you, light will fall onto the entire scene, so everything will be of a similar brightness and should record more or less as you see it. If you're shooting into the light, however, or the sun is to the side of the camera's position, the main part of the scene may be well lit, but little or no light will fall directly onto the frame and it will record dark or even as a silhouette. If the frame and the scene beyond it is evenly lit, you shouldn't experience any problems obtaining well-exposed images. If you're standing in the shadow of the frame, however, overexposure is likely. If this proves to be the case, step beyond the frame and out of the shade, take an exposure reading, set it on your camera using the AE-Lock or by shooting in manual exposure mode, and don't change anything once you re-compose with the frame included. Alternatively, take a shot from your shooting position, check the preview image and histogram, then apply exposure compensation if required and retake.

Finally, if you want the frame and the scene beyond to be rendered in focus, set a small lens aperture, such as f/13, and use hyperfocal focusing to maximise depth-of-field. Alternatively, by setting a wide aperture such as f/4 and focusing on the scene beyond the frame, depth-of-field will be reduced so that the frame itself is thrown out of focus and all attention is directed towards your main subject.

Wide-angle

■ **Lenses: Wide-angle or telephoto?**
The effect the frame has on the composition is partly determined by your lens choice. Wide-angle lenses stretch perspective so the apparent distance between the elements in a scene is increased. If you move close to a natural frame, you can include it in the shot, but you'll still get a clear view of the scene beyond. Telephoto lenses have the opposite effect – they compress perspective so the elements in a scene appear closer together. This makes them less suited to shooting natural frames, though they can be handy at times if you're unable to get close to an effective frame and you're happy for the scene beyond the frame to be more selective.

1) Using archways is something we've seen many times before, but they always lend themselves beautifully to frame a focal point. It works particularly well with this church because the detail in the frame complements the subject.
2) Think about symmetry when looking for natural frames; it is always pleasing to the eye. Even the most simple of arrangements can create impact, as seen here.
3) Using natural frames is a great way of adding foreground interest to a scene. While the castle is the focal point in this image, it's the dramatic spikes that add impact for the viewer.
4) Your subject doesn't have to fill the frame to be striking – here the extra space in fact helps to frame and draw emphasis to the small chapel. Try using subtle but graphic shapes in the landscape such as clouds or hills to improve your composition – simply centring the church would fail to create the same energy as it does here. Think outside the box and you'll begin to see frames in the most unlikely places.
5) The dark frame here is a striking contrast to the lighter scene beyond. Look for differences in colour to emphasise your frame and add impact.

Inspirational Photography Workshops

We work with you
In the class or in the field, we work with you, side by side to make sure you are getting the best out of your time with us and master your photography.

Workshops led by professionals
You will learn from photography masters that are expert tutors and know how to show you what you want to learn in a friendly and practical way.

It's all about you and your photography
We want to help you develop your hobby and passion. Small workshop groups geared towards your level, abilities and interests. The full journey of photography from seeing to printing, in the class or in the field. We have a workshop for you.

Visit www.aspect2i.co.uk or call 0845 505 1455

The Basics **#2**

PERFECT EXPOSURES

DIGITAL CAMERAS HAVE EXTREMELY ACCURATE, multi-zone metering systems, with a histogram function to help us check accurate exposure, so getting it right has never been easier. However, for more creative control, you need to take things into your own hands.

The basic problem is that as we gaze at a beautiful landscape our eyes adjust constantly to register detail in the highlights and the shadows. Our pupils open and close according to the level of light and our optic nerve has impressive range and latitude. Our cameras,

despite their impressive technical specifications, make exposures within fairly limited parameters – the aperture and shutter speed combination will be chosen for the level of light in the scene. A perfectly-exposed sky results in gloomy shadows; detail in the shadows results in a burned-out sky. We need to help our camera to expose the right part of the scene, or find the right balance. The following expert techniques will help you capture perfect exposures by knowing what types of scenes cause problems and what action you'll need to take.

1) Get the balance right

This image presents the landscape photographer with the greatest challenge – extreme light levels with a need to capture detail in the bright sky and the shadows. And don't be fooled by that wet sand in the foreground, it's reflecting a lot of light from the sky.

Of course, it will be possible to manipulate the image on your computer, but first you must make sure the exposure settings capture the maximum amount of information across the whole image. Overexpose and you will lose cloud detail and the blue sky; underexpose and the shadows on the pier will fill-in and become solid. If your digital camera doesn't capture the information, you will have nothing to work with on the computer. There will be an optimum exposure setting but it could be a compromise, so if in doubt, use your camera's bracketing function to take several images, some underexposed and some overexposed.

MARK BAUER

✅ Mid-tone metering

Metering systems in digital cameras are calibrated to an 18% grey mid-tone. Basing exposure readings on a mid-tone such as grass is a good starting point for accurate exposures

2) Getting the right exposure

Mark Bauer was looking for a 'different' view of Corfe Castle in Dorset, so he sauntered along to the graveyard in the village. Having found a composition based around one of the crosses, the next problem was sorting out the exposure. Mark explains, step by step, how he tackled the challenge:

1) This is what the camera's multi-zone meter came up with, without the aid of any filtration. The scene is high in contrast, and the camera has struggled to capture all the tonal information.

2) Spot meter readings from the base of the cross and the sky revealed a difference in brightness of about 4½ stops. Setting an exposure for the land, I fitted a 0.9ND grad filter (three stops) and pulled it down below the horizon, to the edge of the darkest shadow area. I used a soft grad so that it wouldn't cut a line into the cross. As there is some loss of detail in the brighter parts of the sky, I reduced the exposure by two-thirds of a stop and re-shot.

3) The result is that the image has now been 'exposed to the right' (see over the page), without 'clipping' the highlights. The histogram shows that there are still dark tones, but also plenty of information in the top section, and no clipped shadows.

4) A straight conversion of the Raw file looks dull, the picture lacks contrast. For the final version, I've brought the exposure down slightly and added more contrast, especially in the shadows, to recreate the drama of the original scene. I've also tweaked the White Balance to add warmth and increased the saturation too.

5) For comparison purposes, I also took a shot that was underexposed by one stop. As you can see, it's left the shadows muddy and lacking in detail.

Exposure

■ Shadows

These two examples on the right show why it's not a good idea to underexpose and then try to open up the shadows during processing. The nearest image is around one-stop underexposed (to maintain highlight detail) and the shadow curve has been pulled up to match the exposure in the correctly exposed version on the right. As you can see, not only is there 'posterisation' in the shadows, rather than smooth tonal transitions, and tons of noise, but also the sensor has recorded significantly less detail.

3) Exposure for coastal landscapes

Achieving the correct exposure in coastal shots can be a bit trickier than for inland landscapes, as there are several things that can fool the camera's metering system, for example bright highlights on water or bright white foamy waves can lead to underexposure. On the other hand, if you have chosen a large, dark rock for your foreground, this could cause the camera to overexpose. So you need to keep an eye out for any large areas of particularly bright or dark tones and apply exposure compensation accordingly. It is good practice to check the histogram after each shot and be prepared to re-shoot if necessary.

There can also be a huge range of contrast within any one scene, with bright skies, dark rocks, and bright highlights on water. Neutral Density (ND) graduate filters are essential, and depending on the conditions and the brightness of the sky and sea relative to your foreground, you may need to pull the grad down very low in the frame. This could even be below the horizon, to the top of your foreground. If you don't, you might end up with a correctly-exposed sky and foreground with a band of over-bright water in the middle of the picture. So when metering the scene to choose the strength and placement of the filter, remember to take readings from the foreground, sky and sea.

LONG EXPOSURES

■ Exposing to capture movement

One of the great things about taking photos by the sea is the opportunities it gives for capturing the movement of waves and adding atmosphere. In low light, with the lens stopped down to extend depth-of-field, long exposures are a necessity. They may range from several seconds to minutes, depending on lighting conditions. As waves wash around rocks or up and down the shore while the shutter is open, they will record as a romantic, mysterious mist. To capture the drama of waves breaking on the shore, speeds of ¼ sec or slower work well.

4) Histograms: An aid to checking exposure

THE BASICS In simple terms, a histogram is a two-dimensional graph, often resembling a range of mountain peaks, that represents an image's tonal extent. Whilst, at first glance, histograms might appear complex and confusing, they're actually very simple to read. They are an essential aid for digital photographers striving to achieve consistently correct exposures in-camera and are a more accurate method of assessing exposure than looking at images you've taken on the LCD monitor. Therefore, if you're not already in the habit of regularly reviewing your images' histogram, it is time you did so. With our guide, you will soon feel confident assessing histograms.

WHAT IS A HISTOGRAM? A histogram is a visual representation of an image's tonal range. The horizontal axis indicates the picture's extent from pure black (0, far left) to pure white (225, far right). The vertical axis shows how many pixels have that particular value. Looking at an image's histogram, you can tell whether the picture is made up of predominantly light, dark or mid-tones.

Although its appearance is also dictated by the colour and tone of the subject, a histogram with a large number of pixels (or a sharp peak) grouped at either edge is an indication of poor exposure. For example, a histogram with a large number of black pixels (grouped to the left) often signifies underexposure and that subject detail will be obscured in the shadow areas. A large number of pixels grouped to the right of the histogram normally indicates an overexposed image. The image's highlights will burn out (or 'clip') and this detail is irretrievable. A graph with a narrow peak in the middle and no (or few) black or white pixels indicates an image lacking contrast.

SO WHAT SHOULD A HISTOGRAM LOOK LIKE? This is a tricky one to answer. Despite what some people may say, there is no such thing as the perfect histogram. It simply tells us how a picture is exposed, allowing photographers to decide whether – and how – to adjust exposure settings. Therefore, a histogram of a light scene will be very different to one with predominantly black tones or one with a mix of both. However, generally speaking, a histogram should show a good spread of tones across the horizontal axis, with the majority of pixels positioned near to the middle, (100, mid-point). Normally, it is desirable to avoid peaks to the right-hand side of the graph, as this is usually an indication of 'burnt out' (overexposed) highlights, resulting in lost detail.

When assessing a histogram, it is important to consider the brightness of the subject itself. For example, a scene or subject boasting a large percentage of light or dark tones – like snow or a silhouette – will naturally have an affect on the overall look of the resulting graph. Therefore, whilst it is possible to make recommendations, it is impossible to generalise about what is and isn't a good histogram. While an even spread of pixels throughout the greyscale is often considered desirable, you will also need to use your own knowledge gained through experience.

HOW DO I CHECK AN IMAGE'S HISTOGRAM? Most digital SLRs allow you to view the histogram on the LCD monitor during playback. To do this, press the playback button to view the image and then cycle through the additional photo info screens until the histogram is displayed. Make this your default setting so you can quickly access the histogram and assess exposure immediately after taking the picture when required. If the histogram indicates underexposure, apply positive exposure compensation. If pixels are grouped to the right-hand side and the image appears overexposed, dial in negative compensation. Using the histogram is a far more reliable method of assessing exposure than looking at images on the LCD screen, particularly when trying to view images outdoors in bright light when the light reflecting from the LCD can prove deceptive.

Don't panic!

Exposure warnings

The majority of DSLRs are designed with a playback function known as the 'highlights screen'. Whilst histograms provide a graphic illustration of an image's tonal extent, helping you assess exposure overall, the highlights screen – or highlights alert – is aimed specifically at helping photographers to avoid highlights burning out. White or very light subjects in direct sunlight are especially prone to this. A histogram with a sharp peak to the far right will normally indicate that an image is suffering from areas of overexposure. However, the highlights alert actually identifies the pixels that exceed the value for pure white (255). Pixels that do so are not given a value, meaning they cannot be processed and are effectively discarded, having no detail or information recorded. When the image is replayed on the camera's LCD monitor, the pixels falling outside the camera's dynamic range flash or blink providing a quick and graphic illustration of where picture detail is 'burned out' and devoid of detail. To rectify this, set negative exposure compensation so that the next image is recorded darker.

A digital camera's highlights alert is not always switched on by default. Therefore, consult your user's manual and switch it on when you feel this type of exposure warning would prove useful. Normally this is done via the camera's Playback Menu.

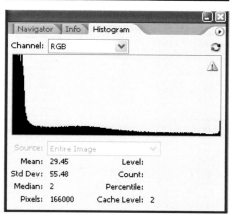

PEAKS TO THE LEFT The histogram is skewed to the left, as the dark backdrop means many of the pixels are in shadow areas, but the image is well exposed.

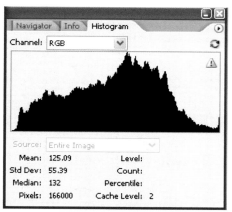

PERFECT EXPOSURE A typical landscape scene gives a so-called 'perfect histogram' as it has a good spread of tones and peaks through the mid-tones.

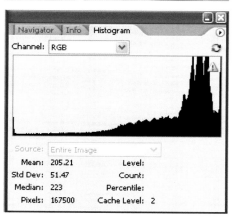

PEAKS TO THE RIGHT A well-exposed shot of an overly-light scene gives a histogram skewed to the right, much like that of an overexposed image.

5) Expose to the right

'Exposing to the right' is fast becoming a widely-accepted approach to help maximise image quality – although it only applies if you shoot in Raw. With this technique you effectively push exposure settings as close to overexposure as possible without actually 'clipping' the highlights. The result is a histogram with the majority of pixels grouped to the right of the mid-point – hence the name 'expose to the right'. So, when you're confident you understand exposures well enough, give this technique a try and push the exposure as far to the right of the histogram as you can, without 'clipping' the highlights. The image will probably look a little light once in the Raw converter, but this is easily corrected with the Brightness and Contrast controls and will give much better results than trying to lighten a darker image.

CCD and CMOS sensors count light in a linear fashion. Most digital SLRs record a 12-bit image capable of recording 4,096 tonal values over six stops. But the tonal values are not spread evenly across the six stops, each stop records half the light of the previous one. So, half of the levels are devoted to the brightest stop (2,048), half of the remainder (1,024 levels) are devoted to the next stop and so on. As a result, the last and darkest of the six stops, only boasts 64 levels. This might seem confusing but, simply, if you do not properly use the right side of the histogram, which represents the majority of tonal values, you are wasting up to half the available encoding levels. So if you deliberately underexpose to ensure detail is retained in the highlights – a common practise among many digital photographers – you are potentially losing a large percentage of the data that can be captured.

MAIN IMAGE & INSET: Exposure to the right of the histogram will capture maximum detail and minimum noise. Once in the Raw converter the image will look too light and washed out so use the Brightness and Contrast controls to adjust the image's appearance.

Aperture-priority is the mode for you!

So what makes aperture-priority mode more useful than any of the other exposure modes for shooting landscapes. Read on – all will be revealed

APERTURE-PRIORITY MODE gets its name because it allows you to decide which aperture (f/number) you want to use to take a photograph, while the camera automatically sets the corresponding shutter speed, based on light levels, to achieve the correct exposure. In other words, it lets you prioritise the aperture selection, and it chooses the shutter speed accordingly.

As the lens aperture is the most influential factor over depth-of-field (the zone of focus) in a photograph, aperture-priority mode is the most practical shooting mode if you are photographing a subject or situation in which control over depth-of-field is important. Landscape photography is the best example. Generally, when shooting landscapes, you'll want to make sure your depth-of-field is broad enough to record the whole scene in focus, from the immediate foreground to infinity, which means that you'll need to set a small aperture, such as f/11. Aperture-priority mode lets you do this easily, because you have to actively set the required aperture.

When shooting portraits, the opposite tends to apply – you want shallow depth-of-field, so that your subject is recorded in focus but the background is thrown out of focus. That means making sure you take the picture with a wide aperture such as f/4 or f/2.8, which again is easy when shooting in aperture-priority mode because it's you and not the camera that decides which aperture to use.

That said, you can still control which aperture is set using other exposure modes, but it just requires a slightly different (and longer) way of working. In shutter-priority (S or Tv) mode, for example, you need to change the shutter speed until the camera sets the aperture you want. In program mode, you can use the program shift function to change the aperture and shutter combination that the camera has set until you get the right aperture.

Where aperture-priority mode triumphs over other modes is that once you've set an aperture, the camera won't change it, even if light levels fluctuate. Instead, the shutter speed adjusts to maintain the correct exposure. This wouldn't be the case if you set the camera to shutter-priority – if light levels change, your camera automatically adjusts the aperture to maintain correct exposure, giving the shutter speed priority, so your control over depth-of-field is diminished. Similarly, in program mode, the camera would change the aperture/shutter speed combination in response to changing light.

Aperture-priority mode is also handy for general use: ie when you're wandering, shooting anything that takes your fancy, such as architecture, details, abstracts or candids. Depth-of-field requirements will vary depending on the shot – one minute you need lots, the next, as little as possible – but you can alter it quickly with the flick of the camera's input dial, and the viewfinder display will keep you fully informed of exactly which aperture (and corresponding shutter speed) you're using.

THE EFFECT OF APERTURES With depth-of-field having such an effect on the final image, it's no surprise that many experienced photographers rate aperture-priority mode as their favourite mode. These two shots show how different apertures can produce very different results.

Setting aperture-priority mode on your camera

Choosing aperture-priority mode is simple – all you need to do is turn your exposure dial (or in some cases push the exposure mode button) and select A or Av. Your digital camera will then be set to aperture-priority mode and all you need to do is rotate the small adjustment dial (found either on the handgrip or on the top-right corner of the rear of your camera) to change your aperture. If you lightly depress the shutter button to activate the exposure system, you can keep a check on the shutter speed the camera has selected.

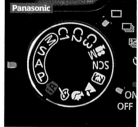

How other exposure modes work

We've already established that in aperture-priority mode, you set the desired aperture and the camera sets the accompanying shutter speed to give the correct exposure. Here's a quick rundown of how the other modes work.

Full-auto mode
The camera sets the shutter speed and aperture to achieve the correct exposure. You can't change the combination to use a specific aperture or shutter speed.

Program mode
Program works in a similar way to full auto, but you can usually alter the aperture/shutter speed combination if you need to use a specific aperture or shutter speed.

Shutter-priority
You set the shutter speed and your camera sets the appropriate aperture. If light levels change, the same shutter speed is used and the aperture changed.

Metered manual
You manually set both the aperture and shutter speed independently of each other, so neither changes unless you adjust them, even if light levels fall or rise.

Subject modes
These program modes are tailored to suit a specific subject, with various camera functions like the AF, flash and exposure systems set accordingly.

Aperture increments

Most cameras allow you to change the apertures in 1/2-stop increments. Check the custom function menu in your camera – many models also allow you to set it to 1/3-stop increments if you so wish

Shot at f/22

Aperture-priority mode allows photographers to control how much of the scene is sharply in focus.

Shutter speeds & landscapes

You need a slow shutter speed when you want to add energy and movement to a landscape image

LANDSCAPE PHOTOGRAPHERS understandably give priority to apertures, but in some situations, shutter speed is just as important to capture the effect of movement within a scene. Because you want to maintain sharpness by maximising depth-of-field, you can make shutter speeds work for you as the smaller apertures you'll require also mean slower shutter speeds. This is easily done by setting your camera to shutter-priority (Tv or S) mode. This ensures you get the correct exposure as you set the shutter speed for the desired length of time, while your camera adjusts the aperture accordingly. So why choose the shutter speed rather than the aperture? Well, setting the slower speed means anything moving when you fire the shutter, such as flowing water or foliage blowing in the wind, is captured as a soft blur, while anything static, like a fence or rock, remains in focus. The effect of setting a long exposure is to give images extra depth and dimension whilst illustrating a sense of movement. The result is usually closer to how you remember the scene, rather than a lifeless image of grass with every blade in focus.

But remember: even digital cameras can be fooled. Be careful not to overexpose an image when shooting, for example, a field of golden sweeping grass in the evening sun. As you lower the shutter speed, the camera's chosen aperture will eventually flash, indicating that the image will be overexposed. You can, of course, check the image and the histogram on the LCD monitor for blown-out highlights.

For even slower shutter speeds and to lift your landscape photography to another level, use filters. A polariser cuts out reflections and darkens blue skies to give clouds that 'wow' factor, as well as reduces the amount of light reaching your sensor by two stops. You can enhance movement and blur by using a Neutral Density filter: a neutral grey filter that doesn't affect colour balance but has the effect of reducing the amount of light passing through it, allowing you to select slower shutter speeds.

For optimum results, shoot at dawn and dusk and use a tripod. Shoot on darker, cloudy days, and let nature work for you – less light means slower shutter speeds. On windy days, hang your camera bag from the tripod to keep your outfit stable, and use a remote release/self-timer and mirror lock-up to avoid contact with the camera during the exposure. Wait for the wind, open the shutter and watch you don't get blown away!

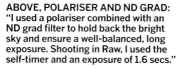

ABOVE, POLARISER AND ND GRAD:
"I used a polariser combined with an ND grad filter to hold back the bright sky and ensure a well-balanced, long exposure. Shooting in Raw, I used the self-timer and an exposure of 1.6 secs."

SHUTTER SPEED COMPARISON:
"The lens (10-22mm set to 13mm) was focused on the grass in the foreground. The only thing I changed was the shutter speeds in a sequence from 1/50sec to 1.6 secs. Note how the grass gets more blurry as the shutter speed becomes slower. My favourite image from the sequence is the longest exposure, which captures the movement exactly as I remember it."

1/50sec

1/20sec

1/10sec

2) Weather and light

In theory, there's no such thing as good or bad weather for landscape photography – good images can be produced in any conditions. Of course, certain conditions will produce more dramatic shots and the trick is learning how to recognise and anticipate them.

If you're planning a sunset or sunrise shoot, don't cancel it if there's cloud cover. If there's a break on the horizon, there's a possibility that the clouds will be lit from below when the sun gets very low, producing a dramatic sky.

Sunshine and showers can be stunning in the moments when the rain stops and the sun breaks through, with foreground objects spot-lit against a dark, brooding sky. These moments are fleeting, however, and don't last for long, so you need to have your camera prepared beforehand.

If the weather is bad – grey, overcast and raining – there are still shots to be made. In these conditions head for woodland: the diffused, less contrasty lighting suits this type of location. Surprisingly, using a polariser can really enhance a picture, by cutting out the reflections and glare from wet foliage as well as saturating the colours.

3) Capture the right mood for the scene

Shoot in lighting conditions that will enhance the natural mood of your subject. For example, some scenes are naturally more tranquil and will look best in the corresponding soft light of dawn and with pastel colours. Others have a naturally brooding atmosphere and demand dramatic, theatrical and directional lighting. And the best light might be months away.

Look at the pictures of the Norman Chapel at St Aldhelm's Head in Dorset on the right. The chapel has a brooding presence, which, as can be seen from these pictures, is best suited to low light and heavy skies.

4) Enhance low light with reflections

Pre-dawn and twilight are very moody times for landscape photography, but the land itself can be almost completely in shadow, with very little detail.

Near water you can include reflections as a foreground, which will help to balance the shot and throw more drama and impact into your image. The more still the conditions the more mirror-like a surface.

With the sun yet to appear above the horizon, the wonderful colours in the sky can be used to add colour and impact into the foreground. The slight breeze of this scene in Mudeford (right) had to drop before the water was still enough to provide this perfectly clear reflection.

5) Backlight for impact!

There's a fancy name for this. It's called 'contre-jour', from the French for 'against the daylight'. If you want to avoid the funny looks, stick with 'backlighting'. Objects are turned to silhouettes, shadows, rays and reflections explode into the lens and create that powerful feeling of being there. Expose carefully, mind, it's tricky.

Spring light

Summer light

Autumn light

Winter light

6) Seasonal light

In winter the landscape is more exposed and the low sun casts long shadows throughout the day. The air has less dust, giving the light clarity. Clear, cold nights lead to frosty mornings with pastel skies.

The light in summer is often less favourable for landscape photography, with the high sun creating harsh light for a large part of the day, with more dust and heat haze meaning the light is generally less clear.

In early spring and late autumn, the light and clarity are better than in summer and it's possible to shoot for most of the day. The weather is changeable, which can create moody and dramatic photo opportunities. In late spring and early autumn, after a cool night, mist can often form at dawn as the land begins to warm up.

BE READY TO GO:
A covering of snow might only last a few hours, even at high altitude. It's a good idea to have a bag packed and ready to go when the weather forecast mentions the white stuff. Time saved not having to hunt for your filters or a charged battery might make the difference between a shot like this (below) and a later one with slushy footprints all over it.

Kit watch!

▨ Keep comparisons in camera

Digital cameras make seasonal comparisons like this set of four, above, much easier. When you revisit a location every three months, carry the previous images on the memory card to help you to recreate the exact distance and crop.

7) Lighting 'on the edge'

A lot of the action in landscape photography happens 'on the edge' – the transition between one state and another. In terms of light, this means the transition from day to night and night to day, the change from one season to another, the transition from calm to stormy weather and so on. Capturing these moments can result in powerful pictures, especially when combined with other themes, such as the boundary between land and water, wilderness and civilisation and so on.

'Edge' themes coming together: the interval between one storm passing and one arriving, the edge of land and water and the transition between night and day.

In the first shot (left), the storm is still clearing as the sun is setting and in the second (above) there was a fantastic afterglow before the next storm rolled in.

The time of day

From the moment first light appears to the time when darkness takes over, the quality of light undergoes a myriad of amazing changes and makes a huge difference to your photographs…

PREDAWN First light usually appears 30-40 minutes before sunrise. Ideally, arrive an hour before sun-up to find a viewpoint, set up your gear and start shooting as soon as colour appears. Any light on the landscape is reflected from the sky, so it's soft and shadowless, and tends to have a strong, cool cast. This contrasts well with the warm glow over the eastern horizon.

Water, wet sand and wet rocks pick up the colour in the sky, so predawn is great to shoot coastal or lake views. Ideally, there will be some broken cloud adding colour to the sky, but clear mornings can also be highly productive. Light levels are low, so expect long exposures. The contrast between the sky and land is high due to the lack of direct light, so use a 0.9ND grad to retain detail and colour in the sky.

SUNRISE By the time the sun peeps over the horizon, any colour in the sky may have gone. On clear mornings, the sun will be dazzling once it rises, but you'll be able to shoot into it for a few minutes as the sea and wet sand reflects the light to keep contrast manageable. Features such as piers, castles and lighthouses can also be captured in silhouette. Inland, contrast will be too high once the sun rises into a clear sky. At this point, turn and capture the golden light on the landscape. Ideally, let the sun side-light the scene so you can include long, raking shadows to add depth and reveal texture. The light is warm at sunrise because the rays pass through the atmosphere at a shallow angle and the light is scattered, with many of the wavelengths at the blue end of the spectrum filtered out.

EARLY MORNING Once the sun is up, you have minutes to capture the light at its peak quality before it loses warmth. During the summer, daylight is neutral in colour two hours after sunrise and its colour temperature remains constant for about 12 hours. During spring and autumn, any warmth in the light will have gone by 8am and the colour temperature remains steady until 4pm. In winter, however, the colour temperature hardly ever reaches 5500K, even at midday, because the angle between the sun and earth is shallow all day.

The first two hours after sunrise are the best for landscape photography as the intensity of the light is reasonably low, and long shadows add depth and modelling. A polariser is also effective when the sun is low in the sky and at 90° to the camera.

THE MIDDLE HOURS Once the sun has been up for two hours, the quality of the light in clear, sunny weather begins to tail off. The higher the sun climbs, the more harsh and intense the light and the shorter and denser the shadows. By 9am in summer, the sun is at its 'zenith' – its highest point – and stays there until at least 4pm. The landscape looks flat, contrast is high and the light isn't attractive. The urban landscape is better suited to strong light: shoot modern architecture, using a polariser to deepen the sky, and look for abstracts and colourful details. In the countryside, capture trees against the sky from a low angle and look for reflections in water. Infrared photography works in harsh light, especially in spring and summer when there's lush foliage around.

LATE AFTERNOON Once the sun begins its slow descent and the light begins to warm up, its intensity is reduced, and shadows become longer and weaker. Shape and character return to the landscape, and the longer you wait, the better it gets. In the morning, the light falls on a cold earth, but in the afternoon, the earth is warm so shadows appear neutral, not cool. The atmosphere is also denser in the afternoon, so light can appear redder than it did at the start of the day. The hour before sunset is often referred to as 'the golden hour' due to the richness of the light. Long shadows reveal texture and modelling to give your pictures depth, and because the sun is sinking and not rising, it's easier to predict how the light is going so you can choose a suitable location.

Everything's rosy
The colours and textures in the sky can be spectacular, especially if you pick the moment as the sun rises above or falls below the horizon.

■ **SUNSET** When a sunset seems likely, get to your location 45 minutes before so you can choose the best viewpoint, get set up and take a variety of pictures as the sun dips. Capture the landscape bathed in golden light. If the scenery is relatively flat, the light will perform its magic literally until the moment the sun sets, whereas in hilly regions, you may lose the sun half an hour before. Shooting into the sun will record anything between the sun and the camera in silhouette: a good technique when shooting water because the sun's glow and colour in the sky will be reflected, creating a backdrop to silhouettes of boats, islands, piers and so on. If flare is a problem, hide the sun behind something in the scene or wait for it to set. If you want to record detail in the foreground, use a 0.9ND grad.

■ **TWILIGHT** Once the sun finally disappears below the horizon, light levels quickly fade and the light on the landscape is again reflected from the sky. If you're lucky, there will be a vivid afterglow in the sky created by the sun as it under-lights the clouds above the horizon, but even this will fade quickly. You'll find that colours are muted, the light is soft, shadows fade and light levels fall away. Head to the water's edge where the pastel colours left in the sky look stunning reflected in lakes and rivers. Or use those colours as a background to silhouettes. Long exposures record movement: the swaying of trees in the breeze, the movement of clouds across the sky, the motion of the sea or water flowing in rivers and streams. Keep shooting until those colours fade.

■ **MOONLIGHT** The moon can be a lovely natural source of light. Winter scenes work well because snow and frost reflect the moonlight. Coastal views also work if you capture the shimmering silver ribbon of light from the moon on the sea. By increasing exposure, you can create surreal shots that look like they've been taken in daylight. They'll look normal, but the light will have a strange quality. You can even try recording star trails in the sky created by the rotation of the earth while the camera's shutter is open. Obviously, exposures will be long in low light, so use a tripod, and keep the ISO low – 400 or less – for high image quality. Whatever you shoot, unless the moon is obscured by cloud, you should keep it out of frame to avoid it recording as an overexposed white smudge!

Get up early for 'magic hour' lighting

Dawn is the best time of day for taking beautiful, atmospheric shots, says landscape expert Helen Dixon

WAKING A COUPLE of hours before sunrise, which is often in the middle of the night, is not most people's idea of fun. But if you're prepared to make the effort, you *will* reap the rewards. Planning is essential. Check the weather forecast and the sunrise times on the internet. And check the tide times if you are travelling to the sea – a low tide is usually the best time to visit. If the light fails to materialise, you can always do beach close-ups.

I try to be on location at least half an hour before the sun rises – if not earlier – because it's often before the sun appears that the real magic happens. This also gives me time to set up the camera and to find the best viewpoint. Don't just look for clear days, it's better to have cloud around as this creates wonderful colours in the sky as the cloud reflects the light of the sun. Try to pre-visit and research your location before the day of the shoot. I use Ordnance Survey maps for detailed information on rights of way and parking. Look for appealing places where there will be opportunities for shots that include foreground interest.

Mist mainly develops during a cold night and it will only linger for a short time during the morning or until the heat of the sun burns it away. Something to bear in mind is that during misty conditions, your camera's metering system will often underexpose the scene, resulting in a dull, lifeless landscape. To compensate, alter the exposure by +½ or +1 stop. Check the histogram on the camera's LCD monitor to make sure you haven't overexposed the scene.

The use of Neutral Density graduate filters is pretty much standard in landscape photography. They help to control the brightest part of the image, which is usually the sky. Early in the day, there is a noticeable difference between the light in the sky and the light on the land.

Be aware of lens flare if the sun is included in the frame. To help eliminate this make sure that your filters and lens optics are spotlessly clean. I rarely use a warm-up filter as these filters normally make any green foliage appear a yellow-brown colour. Instead I set my camera's White Balance to Cloudy or Shade to help warm up the scene. Try to avoid using the Auto White Balance (AWB) setting as you are sure to cool down the light, unless of course this is the effect you want.

There are a number of reasons why I personally prefer dawn light over sunset. I like to capture atmosphere in my shots if I can, and early morning is the best time to do this as you are more likely to have a misty or frosty start to the day. The light is often diffused and softer at this time, but it's also more of a challenge to include the sun in the picture too during the morning than in the evening, because at sunset the pollution levels have risen throughout the day, which helps to diffuse the brightness slightly. Another great advantage of early morning is that it's so peaceful, I rarely see another soul. The world belongs to me – it's so satisfying to watch the day unfold and witness the magical light of dawn.

Once the sun has risen and become too strong to photograph, turn to the side or put your back to the sun, being careful not to cast a shadow in the foreground. Now start using the warm light that's illuminating the land. Light is never static but continually changes – it's the main ingredient that allows us to create something beautiful.

Kit watch!

◼ Helen's magic hour kit
Consider what equipment you will need. An absolute necessity is a good sturdy tripod as at this time of the day you're working with long exposures. I use a Manfrotto MF4 carbon-fibre with 322RC2 head – it's a lightweight but stable support and I can hang my bag from the centre post for extra stability on really windy days.

I always use a remote release but if you don't have one, use the self-timer to stop any vibrations and use mirror lock-up if your DSLR has this facility.

I find my 17-40mm wide-angle zoom and my 70-200mm telezoom particularly useful. These two lenses cover most of my requirements. I use the wide-angle zoom when including plenty of foreground elements. And the telephoto zoom is especially good for compressing perspective and creating layers on misty mornings.

Mirror lock-up

Many digital SLRs have a facility that allows the mirror to be raised prior to the exposure, to minimise shake when the shutter is fired. You'll most likely find this is activated via a Custom Function

SHINING THROUGH
I waited for the sun to rise above the horizon – I used the small clump of trees to help diffuse the sunlight.
Exposure: 0.5secs at f/22.

Stay out late and shoot stunning sunsets

The other 'magic hour' is at sunset – be prepared and you'll be rewarded, reveals Mark Bauer

ALTHOUGH IT'S POSSIBLE to take landscape photographs at most times of the day, there are two times when most landscapers agree the light will give the best results – the first and last hours of the day. What makes these times of day special is that the low sun casts long shadows and helps to pick out the features of the landscape. If you're out pre-dawn or post-sunset, you can also see spectacular skies as the clouds are lit from below.

The light is quite similar at these two times of day, and whether you prefer one or the other often depends on which direction of light will best suit your chosen subject. So, for example, the south coast in winter will look best at the end of the day rather than the start. Having said that, the light in the final hour of the day tends to be warmer, and as the sun sets, the landscape is often bathed in a golden glow. And, of course, the nice thing about sunset compared to sunrise is that you don't have to force yourself out of bed at a ridiculous hour to make the most of it. Let's be honest, not everyone has the willpower and enthusiasm for sunrises as Helen Dixon (see previous page)!

Almost any type of landscape looks good in the magic hour, but some features really benefit, like stone buildings or rocky cliffs. When the low sun warms everything up and picks out the texture of rock and stone, scenes that might look dull at any other time of day can be lifted out of the ordinary.

Water is also an excellent subject at this time, because if you have an interesting sky, you can double the impact by using reflections. Moving water can sparkle like diamonds or be made to blur during long exposures. Again, the amount and type of light falling on it will determine the result.

The direction of the light can have a strong influence on the mood of pictures taken at the beginning or end of the day. Front lighting can look flat, as the direction of the shadows doesn't help to pick out the details of the landscape.

With the sun to one side, shadows help create depth in the picture and reveal form and texture. Side-lighting is best if you want to use a polariser to saturate colours, as it will have its strongest effect if the camera is at a 90° angle to the sun. Backlighting can be very dramatic, but exposure is difficult to control and you will have to be careful to avoid flare as light falls directly onto your filters or the front element of your lens.

So, as weather is notoriously unpredictable, how can you tell if the magic hour will live up to your expectations? Looking at weather forecasts is a good idea. The Met Office's website (www.metoffice.gov.uk) is reliable and you can get a fairly detailed forecast for specific regions. Remember that the longer the range of the forecast, the less reliable it will be. Checking the forecast the night before a dawn shoot gives you the best guide.

If you drive to your location, listen to local radio stations in the car, rather than national ones, and keep an eye on what's happening in the sky.

For sunsets you'll need to look to the west, as this is where the sun will be at magic hour. Most of our weather fronts come from the west, too, so by keeping an eye in that direction, it's possible to see if cloud is likely to break up or thicken.

Being aware of wind direction, the points of the compass and weather patterns will help enormously and you will eventually start to recognise the signs of a magic moment.

Kit watch!

■ Mark Bauer's magic hour kit

Wide-angle lenses are the most popular for landscape work, but longer lenses can also be useful for picking out the kind of patterns and textures that the magic hour reveals.

A polarising filter will help you make the most of side-lighting by improving overall saturation, but is especially effective when used with blue skies.

A sturdy tripod is another essential. If you're shooting in the period after sunset, light levels will be low and hand-holding will be out of the question. But it's good practice to use a tripod whatever the lighting conditions – it will slow you down, it makes you think and it enables you to make small but often vital changes to composition.

Neutral Density graduate filters are also important, especially if clouds are lit from below and there is no direct light on the land. ND grads help control contrast.

White Balance
The White Balance you set has a major effect on the final result. Avoid using the AWB setting. If you shoot in Raw, you can try out all the settings later on your computer and choose your favourite

OSMINGTON MILLS BEACH
The low sun picks out the details of the rocky ledge and gives the cliffs a warm glow. A 0.6ND grad, angled so as not to cut into the cliff, helps retain details in the sky.
Canon EOS 5D with 17-40mm lens.

MARK BAUER

Watch the weather

Changes in weather have an even greater influence on the quality of light than the time of day, so if you want to take stunning shots every time, you need to be prepared to take on the elements

"THERE'S NO SUCH THING as bad weather, only inappropriate clothing," said comedian Billy Connolly, and he was right. If the sun isn't shining and the sky isn't blue, we tend to refer to the weather as 'bad', but photographically, 'bad' can be good because it gives us variations in the quality of light to work with, adds drama and creates atmosphere. So-called 'good' weather is actually not so good for photography because the light is bland and the landscape looks picture-postcard perfect, which gets boring after a while.

Clouds have a dramatic effect on the quality of daylight because they soften and spread it so intensity is reduced, contrast falls and shadows become weaker. Clouds also add interest to the sky, and the sky can make or break a great landscape.

Days when the sky is a blanket of monotonous grey cloud are probably the least exciting for landscape photography as colours appear dull and muted, and a lack of shadows means scenery tends to look flat and uninviting. However, overcast light is ideal for capturing details in the landscape – the patterns and textures in rocks, the smooth shapes and soft colours in sea-worn boulders and pebbles, the rich colours of autumnal foliage or banks of spring flowers. Strong colours look intense in diffuse light because there's no glare to dilute saturation. Dull days are also ideal for slow shutter speed shots of waterfalls – just keep the boring sky out of the shot and you'll get some great results.

White clouds in their many shapes and forms look fantastic against blue sky, and you can make them stand out even more by using a polariser to deepen the blue. Keep the sun to your side for the strongest effect. Watch out for cloud patterns on the landscape, too – they can add an extra element that makes a good scene great, and are easiest to spot if you're shooting from an elevated viewpoint.

Stormy weather creates the most dramatic conditions for landscape photography – dark clouds rushing across the sky, strong winds blowing and momentary breaks that allow sunlight to flood through and illuminate the scene below. You can't plan for such conditions, but if you venture outdoors in stormy weather, there's always the chance that you'll be in the right place to capture them.

If the sun does break through during a storm, the landscape ends up brighter than the sky, which is a reversal of the norm. What this means in practice is that you can get away without using an ND grad as the sky won't overexpose. However, it's still worth using a 0.6ND grad to make the sky look even more dramatic than it really is.

Something else to watch out for in stormy weather is a rainbow arching across the sky. Rainbows are created when the sun shines through falling rain, so if that happens while you're out, turn your back to the sun and check the sky ahead. To reveal the colours of the bow at their best, try and catch it against dark clouds and use a telezoom to home in on part of the bow. Alternatively, use a wide-angle zoom and include the whole bow.

Mist and fog reduce the landscape to soft shapes and hazy outlines. Three dimensions become two and aerial perspective means that tones become brighter with distance. The light is diffuse, shadows don't exist and fine detail is lost. Scenes are simplified and your images should reflect that.

Telephoto lenses emphasise the effects of mist and fog by magnifying the scene and compressing perspective, so they're great for shooting the overlapping forms of hills and mountains, or picking out elements like a single tree or church spire fading into the gloom. If you want to relegate mist or fog to the distance, then use a wide-angle lens – visibility close to the camera will be much better than farther away, so you can capture plenty of foreground detail and let the rest of

Check the web

If you're planning a landscape shoot, whether it's to head out early in the morning for sunrise or to go off into the wilds for a week, use the internet to gather information that will help you make the most of the light. Here are some websites worth bookmarking:

■ **Weather forecast**
www.metoffice.gov.uk
www.bbc.co.uk/weather
www.xcweather.co.uk
www.metcheck.com

■ **Sunrise & sunset times**
www.canterburyweather.co.uk/sun/ukmap.php

■ **Tide times**
www.tidetimes.org.uk/
http://easytide.ukho.gov.uk

■ **Planning your shoot**
A more sophisticated tool is the Photographer's Ephemeris (www.photoephemeris.com). This is available as a free download for both Mac and PC (plus as a paid-for app for the iPhone) and allows you to determine not only sunrise and sunset times for anywhere in the world, any day of the year, but also the angle of the sunrise/ sunset so you can check if the sun's orb will be blocked by a range of hills, say. Moonrise and set times are also provided.

Below left: Far from ruining the image, clouds can add all-important interest to coastal views.
Below right: Simple scenes suit a misty outlook.
Right: Rays of light shining through storm clouds can have a really dramatic effect.

the scene fade away. Dense fog is heavy and damp. It snuffs out colour and turns the world to grey, so you may decide to convert your foggy landscapes to black & white. Mist is more delicate, so instead of destroying colour, it tends to merge all colours together to create very soft hues. Mist is also fine enough to let the light through, so shoot contre jour at sunrise, when you're more likely to find mist in woodland or over water, and capture golden rays of lights bleeding through. Such conditions aren't common, but the quality of light when you get mist and sunrise coinciding is hard to beat.

Sunny

Mist

Stormy skies

Colour temperature and White Balance

The colour of light is referred to as 'colour temperature', which is measured in Kelvin (K). The warmer the light is, the lower its colour temperature, and the cooler the light is, the higher its temperature.

Our eyes adapt to changes in the colour temperature automatically, so natural light always looks more or less white – this is known as chromatic adaptation. The photographic equivalent is your camera's Auto White Balance (AWB) setting. If you use AWB, you will find that it produces pleasing results in most daylight situations, but the White Balance does fluctuate so you may not record the 'colour' of the light as it really is. If you want to do that, you should set White Balance to the Daylight preset, which is 5500K. This is the colour temperature of 'mean noon daylight', so in normal daylight situations, your images will come out looking neutral. However, at sunrise and sunset the light is much warmer (lower colour temperature), so by using the Daylight White Balance preset, your camera will record that warmth. Similarly, if the light is cool, as is often the case during predawn or in bad weather, using the Daylight preset will record that coolness.

Remember, also, that if you shoot in Raw, you can adjust the colour temperature of the image later. So if you don't like the cool cast, you simply get rid of it, or if a warm image isn't warm enough, you can adjust the colour temperature to make it warmer.

7000K

3000K

Conditions	Colour temp (K)	Colour cast (Daylight WB)
Open shade under blue sky	10000K	Very blue
Shade under partly cloudy sky	7500K	Blue
Overcast weather	6000K	Slightly cool
Average noon daylight	5500K	None
Early morning/evening sunlight	3500K	Warm
Sunrise/sunset	2000K	Very warm

THREE SISTERS, DINGLE

Smerwick Harbour is an amazing bay framed by fantastic bluffs at the end of the Dingle peninsula. The picture was made with a Linhof Techno view camera and a Phase One P45+ digital back. Although the aspect ratio of the Phase back is 4x3, I elected to crop this composition as I felt that a square format worked best here.

To balance the sky to the foreground exposure I needed a LEE 0.6 ND hard grad. I often say that the sky is the greatest show on earth, yet it is still necessary to get the exposure on earth right to get the picture to work!

Digital capture using a technical view camera is no easy task. But when everything works well the quality of the resulting prints is quite astonishing. That is why I use LEE filters, which allow me to get it right in camera. Because I often need to make huge enlargements, my filters must match the quality of the Rodenstock and Schneider digital view camera lenses that I always use. With their reliable neutrality and flawless optical clarity I know my LEE filters remain suitably 'invisible'.

Joe Cornish

www.joecornish.com

LEE 0.6 ND
hard grad filter

LEE Filter Holder

Linhof Techno View
Camera, Phase One
P45+ Digital Back,
Rodenstock Digaron-W
40mm, 1/4 sec @ f11

INSPIRING PROFESSIONALS

Tel: (01264) 338599   www.leefilters.com

The Basics #4

SHARPNESS

IMAGINE YOU'VE FOCUSED on an object that is five metres away. How sharp will something be at six metres? Or even five-and-a-half metres? The answer is governed by depth-of-field: the distance either side of the point of focus that is deemed to be acceptably in focus. As long as you control the aperture you are shooting at, you're in control of depth-of-field, and you can use it creatively. There will be occasions when you don't want much of it at all, and you'll get that effect by shooting with a large aperture like f/4. However, for most of the time that you're shooting landscapes you'll want to maximise depth-of-field to get as much of a scene in focus as possible.

Foreground detail is important and has to be in focus, but so does the rest of the scene. This means using small apertures to get good sharpness either side of the focus point. But just consider this last phrase for a moment, and then think about where you might focus when shooting a landscape. Many novice landscape photographers are happy focusing at infinity when shooting a landscape, but don't forget that depth-of-field extends either side of the point of focus. In fact, the area of

depth-of-field extends one-third in front of the focused point and two-thirds behind: in other words, you get more depth-of-field behind the subject than in front of it. Obviously there is no benefit to having acceptable sharpness extending beyond infinity, but you can pull the point of focus back towards you, so it's the end of the depth-of-field zone that is at infinity instead. This way you'll get more of the scene sharp. This is called hyperfocal focusing and has been used by pro landscape photographers for decades. The optimum point of focus for any scene relies on the choice of aperture setting and the focal length of the lens you use – and changes for full-frame and crop-sensor DSLRs! There are calculators and pocket reference tables you can stash in your camera bag, or you can use a dependable rule of thumb that suggests you aim a third of the way into the picture with your lens set to a small aperture. We'll be covering both focusing techniques, as well as providing you with advice to ensure you maximise image sharpness. This includes revealing why using the smallest aperture won't necessarily produce the sharpest results, even though it gives the most depth-of-field!

Focusing with the hyperfocal distance

Lee Frost explains how to use the hyperfocal focusing distance and aperture-priority for super-sharp scenics

ONE OF THE FUNDAMENTALS of successful landscape photography is being able to control and assess depth-of-field to ensure that the image is sharp from front to back.

Aperture-priority mode helps you to achieve this, not only by forcing you to think about which aperture to set, but also by making sure that once it is set, that aperture won't change if light levels fluctuate or you put filters on the lens. If the exposure has to be adjusted when shooting in aperture-priority mode, the camera does it by changing the shutter speed, so the aperture remains constant. This is vitally important because achieving extensive depth-of-field is not just about aperture selection, but also focusing distance, and a careful balancing act between the two is required to ensure the best possible results. You could take every picture at f/22 with the lens set to infinity and most wide-angle shots would be sharp from front to back. Unfortunately, this simple approach won't always work – so you're not going to get the best results. Wide-angles and zooms tend to give their worst optical performance when at minimum aperture and their best around f/11, so ideally you should shoot as close to f/11 as you can to achieve optimum optical quality, and focus the lens at a distance that maximises depth-of-field at that aperture. Over the page, Helen Dixon provides a simple focusing method along these lines that yields excellent results.

My favourite technique is based around something known as hyperfocal focusing, which involves focusing on a point known as the hyperfocal distance, where depth-of-field is maximised for the aperture in use. Lenses used to feature a hyperfocal distance scale on the barrel but virtually none do today. There is an equation for calculating hyperfocal distance for any lens and aperture, so in true *Blue Peter* fashion, I did just that and created a hyperfocal distance chart, which you can copy and refer to when you're on location. The distances in feet (ft) represent the hyperfocal distances for each focal length and aperture. If you focus your lens on that distance and set the corresponding aperture, depth-of-field will extend from half the hyperfocal distance to infinity. So, if you're using an APS-C sized sensor, shooting at 24mm and f/11, focus on a point 9ft away and depth-of-field will extend from 4.5ft (half the hyperfocal distance) to infinity – more than enough depth-of-field in most situations.

TECHNIQUE WATCH!

■ Aperture-priority and multi-zone metering

Before finally 'going digital' back in the spring of 2008, I 'd spent 20 years shooting with film cameras that had no internal metering, so I used a hand-held spot meter to determine correct exposure – which then had to be manually set on the camera. Thankfully, those days are long gone. DSLRs have fantastic integral metering systems that are capable of producing perfectly exposed images in all but the most demanding situations, so I can't see the point in making my life more complicated than it needs to be. These days my digital SLR is set to aperture-priority mode and multi-zone metering and generally stays that way. Combined with the feedback provided by the camera's preview image and the image histogram, I've got all I need to ensure I get perfect exposures in any shooting situation. The same applies to you.

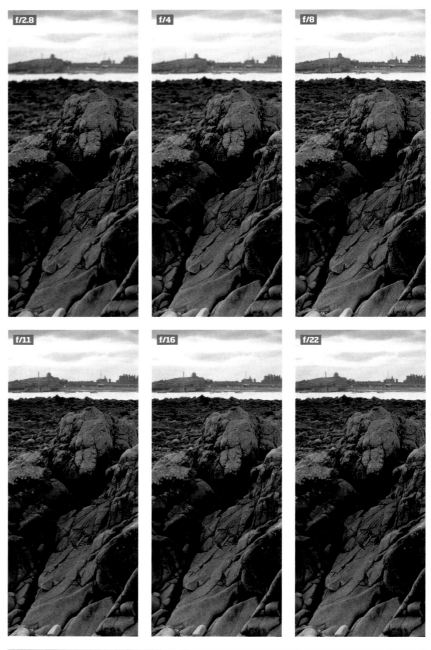

Hyperfocal distance: APS-C sensors										
Focal length	**12**mm	**15**mm	**17**mm	**20**mm	**24**mm	**28**mm	**35**mm	**50**mm	**70**mm	**100**mm	**135**mm
Aperture f/8	3.2ft	5ft	6.4ft	8.9ft	12.6ft	17ft	27ft	55ft	105ft	218ft	395ft
f/11	2.3ft	3.5ft	4.5ft	6.2ft	9ft	12ft	19ft	39ft	75ft	155ft	280ft
f/16	1.7ft	2.5ft	3.3ft	4.4ft	6.4ft	8.6ft	14.5ft	27ft	54ft	110ft	198ft
f/22	1.2ft	0.9ft	2.3ft	3.2ft	4.5ft	6ft	9.5ft	19.2ft	38ft	77ft	140ft

Hyperfocal distance: Full-frame sensors									
Focal length	**16**mm	**20**mm	**24**mm	**28**mm	**35**mm	**50**mm	**70**mm	**100**mm	**135**mm
Aperture f/8	3.8ft	5.6ft	8.0ft	11ft	17ft	35ft	68ft	138ft	250ft
f/11	2.6ft	3.9ft	5.8ft	7.8ft	12ft	25ft	48ft	98ft	178ft
f/16	1.9ft	2.9ft	4.0ft	5.5ft	8.5ft	17.5ft	34ft	70ft	125ft
f/22	0.4ft	2.0ft	2.9ft	3.9ft	6ft	12.5ft	24ft	49ft	89ft

Always use a tripod
If you want to shoot great landscapes in good light, without compromising image quality, mount your camera on a tripod so you don't have to worry about slow shutter speeds causing camera shake

Final image: f/11
If you're an absolute beginner, start off by shooting at f/11 if you can, to optimise image quality, and only use a smaller aperture if you need to get more depth-of-field. How easy is that!

Focus a third of the way in for sharp results!

Ensure depth-of-field and sharpness with this very simple and effective technique, says Helen Dixon

THE NORMAL PRACTICE for beginners shooting landscapes is to place their DSLR on a tripod, focus on infinity and set a very small aperture to give enough depth-of-field to keep most or all of the scene in focus. It's a tried-and-tested method that works well, but can be improved upon by fine-tuning focusing technique and the choice of aperture.

Looking at focusing first, when you focus on 'infinity' – ie on the distance – the depth-of-field will extend a third of the way in front of the focusing point and two thirds behind. So while part of the foreground is sharp, the area closest to you may well be out of focus. Also, you'll have wasted two thirds of the available depth-of-field, which stretches beyond infinity. Instead, by focusing part of the way into the frame, you can maximise depth-of-field so that it covers the foreground and the distance.

The optimum distance at which you should focus is termed the hyperfocal distance and there are various elaborate ways of calculating it. The simplest method for focusing by far (and one that works 99% of the time) is to focus one third of the way into the scene. By doing this, and setting a small aperture, you're ensuring that the depth-of-field in front of the focusing point covers most, if not all, of the foreground, while the area behind is kept sharp by the other two-thirds of the depth-of-field. If you want to be as precise with your focusing as possible, use the table on the previous page.

With the focusing technique taken care of, we'll move onto your choice of aperture. While setting the smallest aperture (eg f/32) gives the most depth-of-field, it doesn't necessarily give the sharpest results. That's due to two main reasons: most lenses are optically designed to give the sharpest results at apertures of around f/8 to f/13, while at smaller apertures the effects of diffraction soften the image, negating any benefits provided by depth-of-field. The optimum aperture varies from lens to lens, so the only way to discover for yourself is through trial and error, shooting at different apertures and comparing the sharpness on your LCD monitor or ideally at home on your computer, where you can magnify images for close scrutiny.

For the sharpest possible results, using the hyperfocal distance method explained by Lee Frost on the previous pages is best. Of course, you must make sure that you set your camera up on a tripod to reduce the risk of camera shake. But this process can be time-consuming and, for most people, my technique is ideal. The images shown here were shot using a fairly dominant foreground to emphasise the effect of changing the focusing distance. The aperture was f/13 for all three images.

TAKING THE SHOTS: Helen sets up a tripod, essential for preventing blurred shots caused by shake, then uses LiveView to check the depth-of-field of the shot on her LCD monitor while selecting the aperture. After taking the shot, she can then check the image's sharpness on the LCD monitor by magnifying parts of the frame.

DON'T PANIC!

■ Blurry viewfinder

When using the hyperfocal distance method, you'll notice that the viewfinder image looks unsharp when you've focused a third of the way into the frame. This is because your lens is always set to the widest aperture to provide a bright viewfinder image – depth-of-field will be minimal. Use the depth-of-field preview button or take a shot at your chosen aperture and you'll see that the image really has far more depth-of-field, because the lens has closed down for the exposure.

Foreground focus
SOFT BACKGROUND
Focusing on the cobbles kept the foreground sharp but the buildings in the distance are soft.

Infinity focus
SOFT FOREGROUND
Focusing on infinity, as many beginners do, gives a soft-looking foreground.

Best method

SHARP SCENE
Focusing a third of the
way into the scene and
using f/13 ensured
maximum sharpness.

How to maximise image sharpness

✔ Set up your camera on a tripod to minimise shake

✔ Focus one-third of the way into the scene

✔ Choose a small aperture like f/13-f/16 to get the best possible optical quality

✔ Check depth-of-field using LiveView

✔ Check image sharpness by zooming in to the image on your LCD monitor

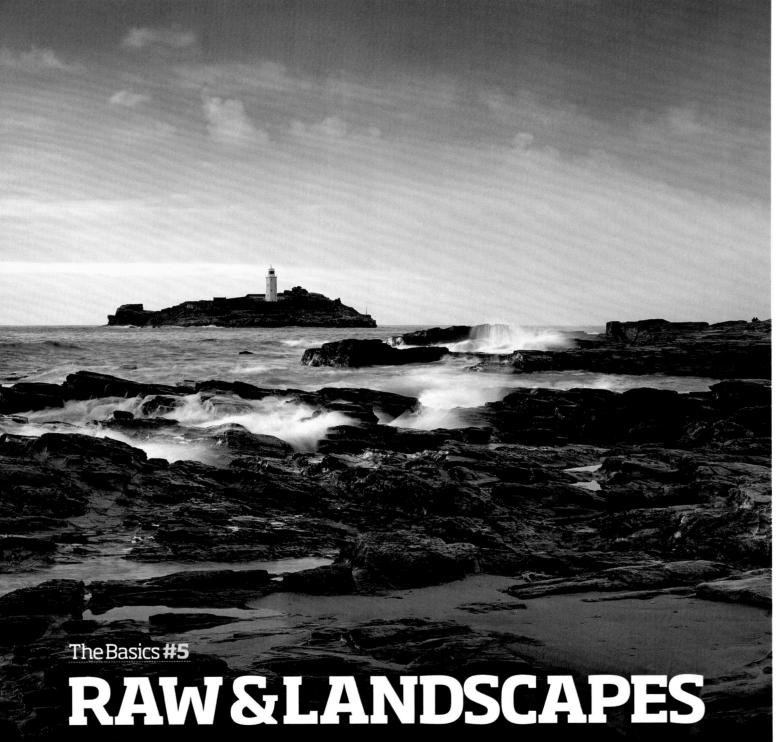

RAW & LANDSCAPES

ALTHOUGH YOU PROBABLY don't realise it yet, producing top-notch images is easier now than at any stage in the entire history of photography, thanks to digital technology. Chances are many of you will have come into photography during the digital era, in which case you'll have little or no experience of what life was like pre-pixels. Well take it from us – taking pictures using digital is a walk in the park compared to shooting film.

Being able to see your shots seconds after taking them is a fast-track to success because you can learn as you go, correcting mistakes and making changes so that you need never miss a great shot. This immediacy, and the fact that every press of the camera's shutter button doesn't cost money, also encourages you to take creative risks, which is by far the best way to master new techniques and fine-tune your skills.

Of course, tripping the shutter is just the first stage in the creative process, as once home your images are then downloaded to a computer where you can turn those millions of coloured dots into amazing works of art with the aid of the latest editing software. Successful digital imaging therefore requires a combination of solid camera work and sympathetic processing.

For many creative photographers, there's only one way to achieve both: shooting in Raw. If you've favoured JPEG until now, and can't see how switching to Raw would benefit you, read on as we explain the many benefits you'll gain going Raw.

An introduction to Raw

If maximum detail and control is what you need, then shooting in Raw is the answer. We cover the basics you need to get started...

THE MAIN DIFFERENCE between a Raw file and a JPEG is that when you shoot in Raw format, the images recorded on your camera's memory card consist of the raw data from the sensor. Nothing is added, taken away or changed. If you shoot in JPEG, the camera records all the raw data then develops the file in-camera; applying pre-set parameters to White Balance, sharpening and custom camera styles etc, deleting any unnecessary information and then erasing remaining raw data as well.

In film terms, a Raw file is a bit like a negative whereas a JPEG is similar to a colour slide. Slides are convenient because they come back from the processing lab finished and ready to view. The same can be said for JPEGs, which are supposedly ready to print straight from the camera. However, this convenience means that you need to get everything right in-camera, so there's less room for error. Negatives are more time-consuming than slides as you need to develop them how you see fit in the darkroom, but are much more versatile with more latitude for error. Raw files are the same. They always require processing using suitable software before they're considered finished, but this allows you to make changes to enhance the images and correct in-camera mistakes. The key parameters you can control in Raw are:
- Colour temperature can be adjusted to get rid of unwanted casts or to change the mood of an image. This can be done with JPEGs in Photoshop, but not with the same precision.
- Exposure can be corrected – or adjusted for creative reasons – without compromising image quality. Whereas if you make a JPEG lighter or darker, image quality will be affected. You can also optimise image quality by overexposing Raw files in-camera to just before the highlights become blown, as shadow detail is increased and the effects of noise reduced. The exposure can then be 'pulled back' while processing the Raw file. This is only possible because the Raw file contains more data than you need, whereas a JPEG is already compressed, so residual data has been deleted.
- If you do accidentally overexpose a Raw file so the highlights 'blow out', you can recover detail during processing. This isn't possible with JPEGs, so blown highlights appear white and if

you try to darken them they simply go grey.
- Sharpening can be applied using the sharpening tools in Raw file processing software or via third-party applications. JPEGs, however, are already sharpened so extra work must be done carefully so not to spoil the images. Any changes you make to a Raw file are non-destructive, because when it's converted to, ideally, a TIFF file, the original Raw image remains unchanged. This means you can return to the same Raw file in the future to process it again. Raw files also contain so much data they can be processed several times then combined either to address exposure and contrast problems, or used as the basis for creative techniques such as HDR (High Dynamic Range), which we'll show you how to do later.

Ultimately, if optimum image quality is what you want, your best chance is to shoot Raw. Raw files support 16-bits of data per colour channel whereas JPEGs support 8-bits. The difference in image quality won't be obvious initially, but heavy editing reduces quality and 8-bit files will show this more readily than 16-bit.

Many photographers are put off shooting Raw as they assume it's complicated. But using Raw processing software is very intuitive (see panel) and any changes you make can easily be reversed or cancelled. A JPEG, on the other hand, while seen as the more convenient format for beginners, actually leaves more room for mistakes, which beginners will surely make.

What are the downsides to shooting in Raw? Well, aside from spending more time at your computer processing files, there aren't many. And if you get as much right in camera as you can, a Raw file can be processed in a matter of seconds. Raw files are around four times bigger in terms of megabytes than JPEGs, so take up more storage space. However, memory cards and external hard drives are cheap these days, so if you've spent a fortune on your camera, it's false economy to choose an image format simply to save on storage space. Bigger image files also mean your camera"s buffer will fill up faster if you shoot in Raw. While this might prove frustrating when shooting subjects such as sports and wildlife, where lots of shots are taken in quick succession, it isn't a real concern for the landscape photographer.

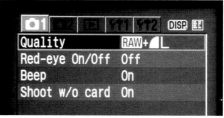

Shoot Raw and JPEG

If you're initially uneasy about shooting Raw, why not set your camera to record every image in both Raw and JPEG? That way, while you get used to processing Raw files, you know you've also got JPEGs of the same images, for reassurance

Shoot & process Raw

Setting your camera to shoot in Raw is easy: simply select the Image Quality setting via the LCD menu screen and choose Raw (or Raw+JPEG). In terms of how you use your camera and its controls, that remains pretty much the same. The only difference is that when shooting Raw, you give the image as much exposure as you can without 'clipping' or overexposing the highlights. By doing this you'll record as much shadow detail as possible and better image quality as a result. It does mean that the images in their raw state appear overexposed, but this is easily resolved during Raw file processing, which you'll find a step-by-step guide for later in this guide. You'll also note that the number of shots you can fit on your card drops dramatically, so carry spares!

Raw processing software

You need special software to process Raw files. When you buy a digital camera, it comes with a CD-ROM containing the camera maker's own Raw processor, Canon has its own system, so does Nikon etc. However, the majority of photographers prefer to use a third-party Raw processor. By far the most popular is Adobe Camera Raw, found in all versions of Adobe Photoshop from CS2 onwards, Photoshop Elements since version 3.0 and all versions of Adobe Lightroom. Apple Aperture also has its own Raw convertor, while Capture One from Phase One is popular with some photographers. SilkyPix is less known but worth trying the free trial download.

- **ADOBE CAMERA RAW**
  www.adobe.com/products/photoshop/family/

- **APPLE APERTURE**
  www.apple.com/uk

- **CAPTURE ONE**
  www.phaseone.com/4/

- **SILKYPIX**
  www.isl.co.jp/SILKYPIX/english/

Troubleshooting

Q I can't open the Raw files from my new DSLR?
That's because camera manufacturers keep changing Raw file formats as they launch new cameras. Adobe release regular upgrades for Adobe Camera Raw (ACR) for new cameras. Go to www.adobe.com and see if the latest upgrade includes your camera.

Q I processed some Raw files and saved them as TIFFs, but the files are really small. What happened?
If you're using ACR, open a Raw file and below the file number for the preview image you'll see a line of text. Click on it and a Workflow Options window opens. Choose Adobe RGB (1998) for Space, 16 Bits/Channel for Depth, 300 pixels/inch for Resolution and for Size, choose the closest size that matches your camera's maximum pixel resolution.

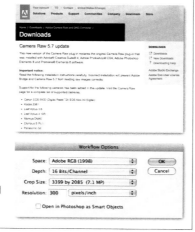

Raw gives you more!
Ever looked at images and wondered how the photographer captured so much detail in the scene? No doubt shooting in Raw played a big part.

The Adobe Camera Raw interface

Faced with a plethora of editing tools and don't know where to start? Find out more about the functions featured on Photoshop CS4's interface

RAW CONVERSION SOFTWARE has an abundance of editing tools that can rescue an image or unleash its creative potential. The margins for adjustment are much wider with a Raw file than for JPEG, due to the sheer mass of information packed in, so the opportunity to experiment without damaging image quality is vast. Here, using Adobe Camera Raw's (ACR) interface, we hope to help you to understand more of the features at your disposal and open your eyes to the power of Raw photography.

While some photographers may do the bare essentials in ACR, and continue processing in Photoshop's main body, you could do most – if not all – of your post-production in Raw if you wanted to. Tools such as Exposure, Contrast, Clarity and Curves are workhorse sliders that you will most likely use every time you open a new image, and therefore we'll address these in our step-by-steps in the next few pages. Instead, here are ten of the lesser known adjustment tools that are well worth learning about...

Top tools to try for Photoshop Raw conversion...

White Balance: Shooting in Raw means you can control the White Balance in post-production, rather than have to select the right White Balance preset in-camera. Under the Basic tab you have all the in-camera WB presets available in a drop-down menu to pick from (e.g. Auto, Daylight, Cloudy etc). You can also use the Temperature and Tint sliders to create your own Custom WB. Alternatively, you could use the White Balance Tool (found in the toolbar) to click on a pure white part of the image, which will then set a benchmark for the White Balance accordingly.

Recovery: This is an image saver for anyone who has slightly overexposed their highlights. This nifty tool should obviously not be relied upon but is definitely one of the most invaluable features in ACR. It can recover mid-tone detail from blown highlights.

Fill Light: Fill Light can be found under the Basic tab and attempts to recover details from shadows, without brightening any blacks. Similar to if you were to use fill-in flash, this tool will cast some light into your foreground – use it with the Blacks slider to add more punch.

Noise Reduction: Under the Detail tab is a section dedicated to Noise Reduction. It is divided into two features: Luminance, (grayscale noise that tends to make an image look grainy); and Color that copes with Chroma noise. To see the effects, enlarge your image to at least 100%.

Vibrance and Saturation: This tool is an alternative to the Saturation slider, which adjusts all the colours in an image equally. The Vibrance tool on the other hand affects colours that need boosting, having less affect on the colours already high in saturation.

Split Toning: Give your shot a completely different look using this traditional darkroom treatment of tinting the highlights and shadows. You can do this simply by selecting the Split Toning tab and then moving the applicable Hue slider to change the colour and the Saturation slider to set the intensity. Don't neglect the Balance slider either as this will allow you to put more emphasis on the intensity of the shadows' tint or the highlights' tint, depending on which direction you move it.

Lens Vignetting: Found under the Lens Correction tab, this is a corrective and creative tool that allows you to darken or lighten the edges of an image. As light fall off is a lens defect that causes the corners of an image to darken, some photographers prefer to correct it. But others like to enhance the effect, making it stronger. You can control the mid-point, feather and roundness of the vignette with this tool.

HSL: (Hue, Saturation and Luminance). The controls on the HSL/Grayscale tab allow you to target specific colours in a similar fashion to Photoshop's Selective Color. Use the Hue slider to change a colour, the Saturation to alter its purity and Luminance for brightness. It's a good idea to increase a colour's saturation and decrease its luminance, rather than just pump up the saturation.

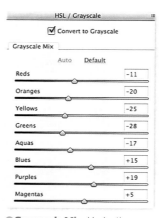

Grayscale Mix: Under the HSL/Grayscale tab you have the option of checking the Convert to Grayscale box, which brings up a new set of tools labelled Grayscale Mix. As well as an Auto option, you can take control over the tonal range of your b&w conversion by adjusting the level of each colour's tone in your original image.

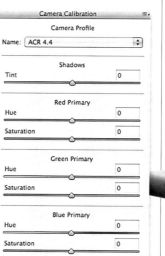

Color Rendering: By selecting the Camera Calibration tab, you can pick from a selection of your in-camera profiles to apply to your image. Locate the different profiles such as Neutral, Vivid, Landscape and Portrait by clicking the drop-down menu labeled Name.

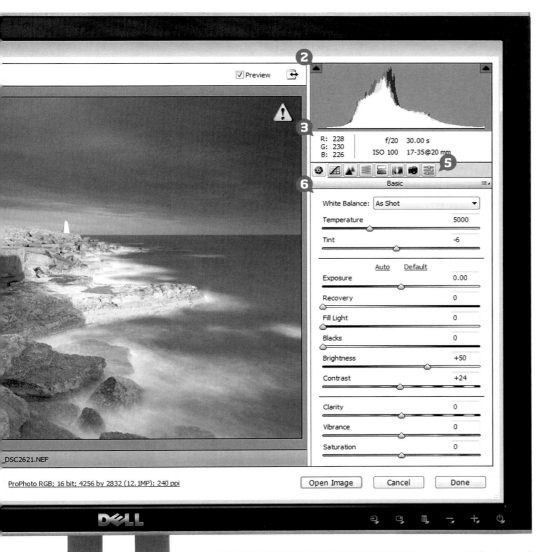

ProPhoto RGB; 16 bit; 4256 by 2832 (12.1MP); 240 ppi

Open Image | Cancel | Done

DSC2621.NEF

✓ Camera compatibility

You may find your new camera doesn't work with Adobe Camera Raw and that's because camera manufacturers keep changing Raw file formats as they launch new cameras. Adobe release regular upgrades for ACR. Go to www.adobe.com for the latest upgrades

Window of opportunity!

While you experiment with the features, you can judge their effect on your image by viewing it in the large preview window on the left.

Raw interface

■ CS4 Features all the tools of CS3 with the addition of an Adjustment Brush and Graduated Filter, found on the toolbar. The Adjustment Brush is the niftier of the two, allowing you to make very specific adjustments to selected areas of the image depending on the size and radius of the brush you decide to set.

■ CS5 As well as a few new fine-tuning sliders to Noise Reduction and the addition of an Effects tab, which allows you to add grain to your image, the toolbar now has a Targeted Adjustment control for photographers who find working directly on an image more intuitive. Users can control the adjustments directly on the image by dragging their cursor up or down to increase or decrease the effect, respectively.

Camera Raw interface

Open a Raw file in Photoshop and you're presented with the following interface. Here we explain the main commands that are displayed:

1) TOOLBAR Contains all selectable tools such as Zoom Tool, White Balance Tool, Hand Tool and Crop Tool. Users of the latest version of Photoshop also have access to the Adjustment Brush and Graduated Filter. Like the main Photoshop program, all the tools have single letter keyboard shortcuts that are worth getting to know. Check the back page for more details on what these are.

2) HISTOGRAM The histogram tells you exactly what is happening to your Raw information in real time as you alter the dialogue controls. It takes the form of a graph, representing colour in numbers from 0 to 255, going from left to right, darkest to lightest. The white shade represents the combined red, green and blue channels and gives you the foremost indication of exposure.

3) INFO PALETTE Shows the pixel readings for Red, Green and Blue channels from 0 to 255 when the cursor is placed in the main window, and also contains image metadata information such as aperture in f/stops, shutter speed in seconds, ISO rating and focal length used.

4) IMAGE WINDOW The main preview window for the open image. You can zoom in using the Zoom Tool or the plus and minus buttons or drop-down menu underneath. You can also move around the image using the Hand Tool or by holding down the Spacebar and dragging. Check the Preview box to see your image with and without current edits.

5) CONTROL TABS You can negotiate between the different control tabs by clicking on each of them. The first tab is labelled Basic and contains the controls that you will use most often, such as the Exposure, Recovery and Blacks sliders. Other tabs are Tone Curve (like Curves), Detail for sharpening, HSL/Greyscale for colour, Split Toning, Lens Corrections, Camera Calibration and Presets. Elements users have only Basic, Camera Calibration and Presets.

6) CONTROL WINDOW This is the main dialogue window that contains the controls for each of the specific control tabs. They're all slider based, other than the Point Curve section of the Tone Curve tab (which allows you to plot points on a curve) and the Preset tab, which involves simply selecting listed Presets.

7) OUTPUT BUTTONS Along the bottom you'll find all the buttons for doing what you choose once you have finished your edits. You can Save, Save As, Open, Open a Copy or use Done to store your edits without actually processing the Raw file. Holding down Alt/Option gives you access to the extra options.

How to process a Raw file

Get the most from every image by processing in Adobe Camera Raw

THE BEST THING about shooting in Raw is that you can process the file to give a far better result than if you had captured the scene as a JPEG. The preview of a Raw file on your camera's LCD monitor may look identical to a JPEG as all the additional information is hidden within the file, and it's impossible to display on your camera's screen. It's only when you open the Raw file on your computer that you'll see the wonders retained in this purest of image file formats. Our step-by-step guide shows how processing Raw files in Photoshop's Adobe Camera Raw allows you to extract an amazing amount of information from a Raw file that leads to a far superior result than if the image had been captured in JPEG.

1 OPEN THE FILE The first thing we do when we open our Raw file is to see how the histogram looks with the default Camera Raw settings. We can see here that contrast is fairly low with the bulk of the information for this image sitting in the middle. The image looks quite muted and would benefit from extra contrast to add colour and detail.

2 ASSESS THE HIGHLIGHTS First check if there's any highlight detail that might be clipped by clicking on the triangle on the top right of the histogram to turn on the highlight clipping display. When active, any clipped areas flash red. The whites of the distant lighthouse here are clipped, which means we might potentially lose some highlight detail.

3 RESCUE THE HIGHLIGHTS You can recover this highlight information using the Recovery slider, but this would be at the expense of highlights elsewhere, which would effectively reduce contrast. The small amount of clipped information isn't that important, so we decide to leave things be. Exposure looks spot on so we don't need to adjust this slider either.

4 BOOST THE BLACKS The image probably looks a little flat straight from the camera, like this one does. Adjust the *Blacks* slider until the histogram spreads towards the far left side by holding down *Alt/Option* and moving the *Blacks* slider until areas show up black on the white background. You've now created the pure blacks in your image, but be careful not to overdo it.

5 WATCH FOR CLIPPING You'd normally look to avoid clipping any highlights or shadows, but sometimes it's necessary in order to strengthen the dark tones and improve contrast. For instance, here we wouldn't expect to see detail in the rock face cracks. We also set *Contrast* to +60 to boost contrast further without clipping too much more shadow detail.

6 BOOST THE COLOUR Now use adjust the *Vibrance* slider (here we set it to 30), or the *Saturation* slider if your software doesn't feature Vibrance, to pump up the colour a little. Press I to access the White Balance Tool and check that you have got the correct White Balance by clicking on a neutral white or grey area – the lighthouse is good here.

Final image
It's clear to see the benefits of shooting your images in Raw, as it's possible to extract far more detail than if you had taken the shot as a JPEG.

7 ADJUST THE WHITE BALANCE If you're not happy with the image's colour tone (White Balance), adjust the *Temperature* slider a little. You can strengthen contrast a little further if you feel it's necessary by clicking from the *Basic* tab to the *Tone Curve* tab. Select *Point* rather than *Parametric* and change the drop-down menu from *Medium* to *Strong Contrast*.

8 ADD IMPACT For this image, we want to emphasise the sky and sea a little more with a selective Saturation and Luminance increase. We chose the *HSL/Grayscale* tab and selected the *Saturation* sub-tab and set *Blues* to *+40*. We then chose the *Luminance* sub-tab and set *Blues* to *+40* here too. As you can see, these tweaks all result in the image delivering far more impact.

9 SHARPEN THE IMAGE Next it's time to negotiate the Detail tab and use the Zoom buttons to zoom in to 100%. Work with the *Sharpness* slider to get the image looking crisp on screen. We settle on Amount 100, *Radius* 1.0 and *Detail* 30. Sharpening too excessively can cause *artefacts* and noise to appear, which is why it's important to take picture at the lowest ISO rating possible.

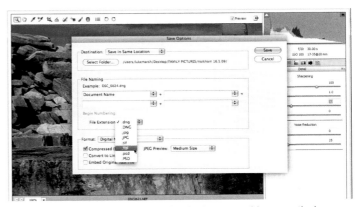

10 SAVE AND OPEN Once you're finished, you can either open the image to continue enhancements in Photoshop or save it for later. By saving the image as a .TIFF or .PSD format you will leave yourself with a 16-bit file as opposed to compressing the image to an 8-bit JPEG, which reduces the amount of information and thus flexibility when editing in the future.

Combining Raw files

Merging two shots is an easy route to perfect exposure. Here's how…

SETTING YOUR CAMERA to shoot in Raw means you can recover hidden detail from areas of a scene that are over- or underexposed. One way to do this is to create two separate images of different exposures from the same Raw file – one for the sky and the other for the foreground – then combine them for the perfect result. In this step-by-step you'll learn how to adjust exposure post capture, how to use the High Pass filter for sharpening and how to make colour adjustments. This technique is especially efficient as you are only working with image data captured in a single exposure, so you can revisit any of your old Raw files to try it. We used Photoshop Elements, but CS works in a similar way.

Raw file

1 OPEN THE FILE When you open a Raw file in Elements the image appears in the Raw control window (above). As the foreground in the original Raw file is well exposed, little work is needed at this stage on the image. Simply click Open, leaving the settings as they are, then go *File>Save As* and create a Photoshop file (*.psd*) as we are going to be working with layers.

2 REPEAT Reopen the original Raw file, and again the Raw control window appears with the image. This time use the *Exposure* control (circled) and move the slider left to underexpose the image, pulling back the hidden detail from the original Raw file's overexposed sky. When you're happy with the results, click *Open* to take the image into Elements.

3 COPY & PASTE You now have two files open. One contains the original exposure and the other is the new underexposed image. With the underexposed file active, click *Select>All* then *Edit>Copy*, placing the image into the pasteboard memory. Now you can close this file and use *Edit>Paste* to place this image into a new layer on the original file.

4 REMOVE FOREGROUND With the two exposures in place, we now want to combine the correctly-exposed foreground with the newly-exposed sky. With the sky layer active and using the *Rectangular Marquee Tool*, select a large area of foreground, just short of the horizon. Next, click *Edit>Delete* to remove the area, noting the effect in the Layer palette preview (inset).

5 CLEAN UP Now it's time to tidy up the horizon, so with the *Eraser Tool* set to a medium-sized, soft-edged brush and the *Opacity* set to around 55%, gradually erase areas of the newly-exposed layer along the horizon, revealing the original foreground image. The slight feathering between the two layers creates a misty effect that enhances the image's mood.

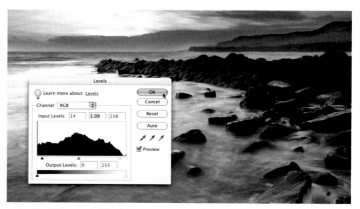

6 ENHANCE The initial layer work is complete, so to save your work so far, go to *Layer>Flatten Image* then *File>Save As* to create a new file. With both layers merged, it's time for some overall enhancement, so click on *Enhance>Adjust Lighting>Levels* to lighten up the image and improve the definition. Click *OK* to apply the changes.

Final image
Stormy skies overhead! It's clear to see the benefits of shooting your images in Raw, as it's possible to rescue more detail than if you'd captured the scene as a JPEG.

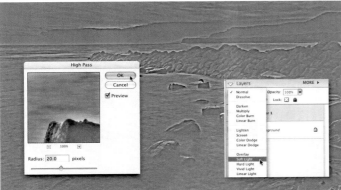

7 HIGH PASS The High Pass filter is a far more forgiving way to enhance detail than sharpening. To use it, first go to *Layer>Duplicate* Layer to preserve the original image. Then go to *Filter>Other>High Pass*, adjusting the *Radius* to around 20 pixels before clicking *OK*. Now you need to change the Blend Mode in the Layer palette to *Soft Light*.

8 DARKEN AREAS Use *Layer>Flatten Image* again, saving a copy if required. Now, using the *Burn Tool* (inset) with a large soft-edged brush and the *Opacity* set to approximately 25%, darken the exposure of specific areas, which helps to improve the depth of the image. Focus on the edges of the frame and gradually build the effect up.

9 SELECT THE SKY The image is predominately blue in hue and we'd quite like to inject a different tone to the sky area. Using the *Rectangular Marquee Tool*, select the area above the horizon and *Select>Feather*, entering an amount of 50 pixels to soften the selection, before clicking *Edit>Copy* then *Edit>Paste*, placing the selection into a new layer.

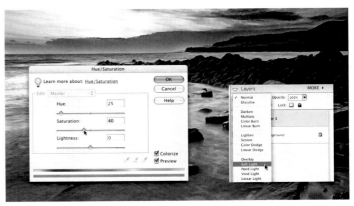

10 ADJUST COLOUR Change the Blend Mode of the new layer to *Soft Light*, and then go to *Enhance>Adjust Colour>Adjust Hue/Saturation*. In the window, start by clicking the *Colorize* box and immediately see the effect in the preview. Finally, adjust the *Hue* and *Saturation* sliders until you are happy with the colour, and then click *OK*.

'Exposing to the right' with Raw

For the full benefits of shooting in Raw, you need to understand how your camera records tonal information and how to read its histogram

TO MAKE THE MOST of a Raw file, you need to learn to use your camera's histogram. Most enthusiast photographers rely on the preview image to judge their exposure, but it's not the best reference. A histogram, on the other hand, provides all the essential information you need to create the ultimate Raw file. It shows the distribution of tones in a digital image, from the darkest shadows on the far left of the histogram to the brightest highlights on the far right. The shape of the tonal graph and its position between the two extremes says a lot about the image: if it's high or low contrast, consists mainly of light and dark tones, is over or underexposed, and so on.

The general rule when exposing an image is to make sure tones fall within the extremes of the histogram to retain detail. If too much information is to the far left, some shadows may lack detail, and if it's to the far right, some highlights may blow out and record as pure white. Making sure neither extremes are 'clipped' gives an acceptable Raw file to work on.

However, if you want to record maximum tonal detail, you need to 'expose to the right'. This involves exposing the image as best you can without 'clipping' the highlights, creating a histogram that's shifted towards the right side. Why? Because sensors record more tones in the highlights than the shadows.

Most sensors record a brightness range of five or six stops. The histogram in many cameras is divided into five sections which, for the benefit of this technique, represent the five stops in brightness it records. Rather than the tonal values being divided equally across those five stops, 50% of the total number are recorded in the brightest stop, half this number in the next, half as many again in the next stop, and so on, meaning that the brightest 20% of the histogram, on the far right, contains 16x more tonal values than the darkest 20% on the far left. By 'exposing to the right' so that the tonal graph extends into the brightest 20% of the histogram, you're maximising the information recorded. When you check the preview screen, images that are exposed to the right look overexposed, so your natural reaction is to reduce the exposure and then reshoot, but ignore the preview and trust the histogram! You can then adjust the exposure and contrast when you process the file, retaining the important tonal values and giving a more detailed image with less noise. As you'll see, darkening an overexposed Raw file is better than lightening one that's underexposed – so long as you don't blow out the highlights.

Increasing the exposure

The easiest way to 'expose to the right' is to take a test frame and then assess the histogram. If the graph is centred, (i.e. well exposed) or to the left, increase the exposure by + 1/3 stop via exposure compensation, take another shot and check the histogram. Repeat until the highlight warning starts to flash on the preview image, indicating that the highlights have been 'clipped' and that you've taken the exposure too far. The frame before, where you gave 1/3-stop less exposure, is the file to work on.

A) This is what the histogram for an underexposed image looks like: the tonal graph is pushed over to the left where there are fewer tonal values. If you took a shot like this and tried to 'rescue' it, you'd have noise problems.

B) There is nothing wrong technically with this image or histogram: the tonal graph is central and neither highlights or shadows have been 'clipped'. If you saw this shot on the preview screen, you'd probably be happy. However…

C) Exposing to the right will record far more tonal values in the Raw files than correctly exposing it. This is what the preview image will look like if you do: overexposed and washed out. But it's the best Raw file of the three!

1 **WATCH OUT FOR 'CLIPPING'** The brightest highlights in the water and sky have been exposed to the point that they've started to 'blow-out' – indicated by the red highlights. The image looks generally washed out.

2 **RECOVER HIGHLIGHTS** Although you should try to avoid 'clipping' the highlights, you can use the *Recovery* slider to rescue them – but no more than about 20% should be applied as it tends to flatten the whole image.

3 **REVEAL THE DETAIL** Various controls can be used to tone down the image – *Contrast, Brightness, Exposure* – but the *Tone Curve* sliders are most effective. Here, the *Dark* tone was moved to -39 and it looks better already.

4 **ADJUST TONALITY** The *Highlight* slider was moved to the right to a value of +26 and the *Lights* slider to the left to a value of -14. You can see how the *Tone Curve* has changed from a straight line to a shallow 'S' shape.

5 **IMPROVE THE COLOURS** Clicking back on the *Basic* tab, the *Blacks* slider is moved to the right to a value of 14 from its default setting of 5, while *Vibrance* is set to +22 and *Saturation* to +8 to boost the colours in the image.

Final image
After saving the processed Raw file as a 16-bit TIFF, a few final tweaks were made in Photoshop and here's the finished image – rather more impressive than the original Raw file it came from.

The Basics #6

FILTERS

Lee Frost reveals the importance of filters for landscape photographers

IMAGINE YOU'RE ABOUT to be shipwrecked on a desert island and the captain of the vessel has given strict instructions that you can only take three filters overboard with you. Okay, so it's a rather extreme scenario, but – hey – worse things have happened at sea! The question is, which three would you take?

As a child of the Cokin era, I managed to amass more filters than your average camera shop. I had bits of plastic (okay, okay C39 resin) that could add fake rainbows to my images, ruin a perfectly nice sky by turning it tobacco, reduce attractive scenes to impressionistic smudges, turn bright points of light into brilliant explosions of colour, and perform all sorts of other weird and wonderful tricks. I never used the things, of course, because most of the effects were horrible. But you weren't a proper photographer unless you carried at least a dozen of them everywhere, and if the worst came to the worst, they were ideal for making a sow's ear from a silk purse. I've got hundred of examples to prove it.

Fortunately, after numerous failed attempts I managed to kick my Cokin addiction, so out went all the filters that weren't essential – which actually left very few. Later still, I jumped on the digital bandwagon, which meant I could jettison even more (mainly the colour correction and conversion filters that have been replaced by White Balance and colour temperature adjustments).

Today, I'm left with only three filter types: Neutral Density (ND) grads, a polariser and solid Neutral Density (ND) filters. For landscape and general photography, they're all you need, and all three can be used individually or in combination to help you get the most from a scene.

Some of you may be thinking, 'Why bother with filters at all when the effects can be added in Photoshop?' Well, if you're thinking that, chances are you've never used them, because while the effects some filters have can be replicated in Photoshop, others can't. And anyway, even if they could all be, surely it's better to get your photographs as close to completion in-camera as possible, rather than spending ages at your computer trying to sort them out in post-production?

For information on filter systems, take a look at the panel below, then read on to see the difference my three favourite filters could make to your landscape images.

Which filter system?

Screw-in: These high-quality glass filters screw directly onto the filter thread of your lens, making them fast and easy to use. You'll find numerous polarisers and ND screw-in filters (including B+W's ten-stop ND) but virtually no ND grads. While offering excellent optical quality, screw-in filters have one big disadvantage: if you have numerous lenses, you'll most likely need to buy several sizes of screw-in filters. Brands to consider include B+W, Hoya, Kood, Jessops and Tiffen.

Slot-in: Your best bet is a slot-in system. You buy rings that screw on to your lenses and a single holder that slips on to these rings – this way you only need one filter. Polarisers, NDs and ND grads are all available as slot-in filters. Cokin (P or X-Pro) and Formatt (Hitech) are good first systems, while Lee Filters is the professionals' choice.

Another fine mist
Mystery, drama, atmosphere... using filters in your photography can make your good shots great.

NDgraduate

Make bland skies a thing of the past by using a Neutral Density graduate filter

HOW MANY TIMES have you composed a great shot with a dramatic sky only to discover that when you check the picture you've taken the landscape looks fine, but the sky is overexposed and washed out?

Naive photographers shrug their shoulders and think, 'Oh, I'll rescue that later', which is fine if there's something to rescue. But if the sky's so overexposed that no detail has recorded, there won't be. More experienced shooters take two photographs of the scene – one exposing for the sky, the other for the landscape – then combine them in Photoshop. This method works well, but does mean more time at the computer. However, the quickest and easiest solution is to use an ND grad filter.

ND grads are grey on the top half – that's the Neutral Density part – and clear on the bottom half. The idea is that the grey part of the grad tones down the brightness of the sky so that when you expose for the landscape, the sky is also correctly exposed instead of being completely blown out.

ND grads & exposure

Before multi-zone metering, exposure readings had to be taken and set manually on the camera before you placed an ND grad on the lens, otherwise it would result in an overexposed image. Metering systems are now so clever that you can compose the shot, align the grad ready for use and meter with it on the lens. This is because a multi-zone pattern takes a number of exposure readings from different parts of the image area, so the darkness of the filter doesn't influence the final exposure set in a negative way. In fact, it helps your camera obtain an accurate reading, as when an ND grad is fitted, the Neutral Density part of the filter darkens the sky area so that the contrast between the sky and foreground is reduced.

Technique watch!

◼ Choose the right density

To produce a convincing result you need to choose the right density of ND grad. Fortunately, making the right choice isn't difficult as there are only three main densities to choose from: 0.3, 0.6 and 0.9, which reduce the brightness of the sky by one, two and three stops respectively. Some manufacturers also produce a 1.2ND grad, which tones down the sky by four stops. The weakest, 0.3ND, is only of use when you need a very subtle effect, while the stronger 0.9ND is mainly used at dawn and dusk when the sky's really bright but there's no direct light on the landscape. That just leaves the 0.6ND grad, which is the best choice for general use. If in doubt, take a test shot with a 0.6ND grad, check the image on your camera's preview screen, then switch to either a 0.3ND or, more likely, a 0.9ND, if the effect isn't right.

Experienced landscape photographers consider an ND graduate as an essential item and not an optional accessory.

ALL IMAGES LEE FROST

Aligning an ND grad

The key to success with a grad is correct alignment, so it does its job without leaving tell-tale signs. Many photographers struggle and assume there must be a magic formula, but it's just a case of taking your time.

1 Mount your camera on a tripod, compose the scene as you want to shoot it. Next, place an ND grad filter in the filter holder on your lens, and while peering through the viewfinder, slowly push the grad down in the filter holder.

2 As you slide the grad down you should see the top part of the picture appear to get darker. It won't be blatantly obvious, even if you're using a strong ND grad, so watch carefully and when you think you've got the ND grad in the right position, stop moving it down.

3 A common mistake is to push the grad too far in to the holder. This means the grad will behave like a 'solid' ND filter and cause an exposure increase, but the sky will still be overexposed and you may see the line of the grad in the foreground.

4 If you are struggling to align the grad by using the viewfinder, try LiveView instead. You may find it much easier to do this as you're seeing the exact effect the filter is having on the image so it's easier to accurately align it.

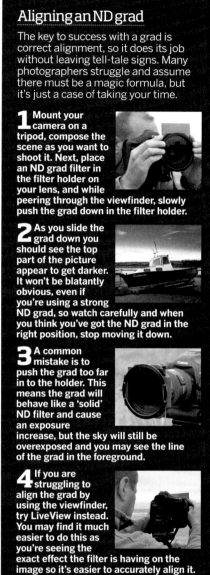

Technique watch!

■ Hard or soft grads?

There are two types of ND grad: Hard and Soft. This refers to the way in which the Neutral Density (grey) part of the filter graduates down to clear – with hard grads the change is quite sudden, whereas with soft grads it's gentle. Newcomers to ND grads assume that soft grads are easier to use because if you align them incorrectly it's less likely that you'll see the line of the grad in your picture. However, hard grads are quite forgiving and also give a more defined effect, so they're the best choice.

Soft

Hard

Soft   Hard

Polariser

A circular polariser will be your best friend, boosting colour impact and reducing reflections

WHEN LIGHT STRIKES a surface, some of the rays scatter in all directions and become polarised, causing glare that reduces colour saturation – particularly on shiny surfaces such as paintwork and foliage – and reflections. Polarising filters prevent this by only allowing light rays to enter your lens that are travelling in one direction, so the polarised light is effectively blocked out. Doing this offers three distinct advantages for landscape photography.

The most obvious benefit is that blue sky is deepened, because it contains a lot of polarised light. Using a polariser allows you to add visual impact to images by providing a strong, punchy blue backdrop. Another benefit is that glare on non-metallic surfaces is reduced, so the colours in a scene appear richer and more saturated. The third advantage to using polarisers is that reflections are eliminated, so you can see through windows and into rivers.

No filter

With polariser

Using a polariser is easy because you can see the effect it has simply by rotating it slowly in its mount on your lens while looking through the camera's viewfinder. Blue sky goes darker and white clouds stand out, reflections come and go, glare disappears. When you're happy with what you see, simply stop rotating and fire. To get the best possible results, however, you should also bear in mind certain factors.

Although polarisers generally work best in bright, sunny weather when there's more polarised light around, they can be used in dull, overcast conditions too in order to remove glare and reflections. Autumnal woodland scenes usually look much better if you shoot them through a polariser, as glare is reduced, so the rich colours of the foliage really come through.

When using a polariser to deepen blue sky, keep the sun at a right angle to the camera so you're aiming towards the area of sky where maximum polarisation occurs. That way, you'll get the strongest effect. If the sun is behind you, or you're shooting into the sun, a polariser won't make much difference. Polarisation in the sky also tends to be better when the sun is low in the sky – so early morning and evening give better results than in the middle of the day.

Polarisation is uneven across the sky, so take care when using ultra wide-angle lenses or zooms with a focal length wider

Polarisers & exposure

Polarisers reduce the light entering your lens by two stops. This means if you have an exposure of 1/125sec at f/11 without a polarising filter in place, the exposure would drop to 1/30sec at f/11 once you fitted it. Your camera accounts for this light loss automatically, so you don't need to compensate, but you need to be aware of it because the shutter speed can easily become very slow when using a polariser – even in bright sunlight – so the risk of camera shake is increased. That said, this light loss can be a benefit when you want to use a slower shutter speed, as the polariser acts like a 0.6-density ND filter (covered overleaf). When shooting waterfalls, for example, the polariser not only gives you a slower shutter speed to blur water but also removes reflections from water and glare from wet rocks and foliage.

Technique watch!

■ Circular or linear

There are two types of polarising filters available: linear and circular. You need to use a circular polariser as linear polarisers are used on certain older non-autofocus film SLRs. Both types do exactly the same job, but a circular polariser is manufactured differently to ensure correct exposure when used with autofocus DSLRs and CSCs.

than 24mm (16mm on APS-C sensors) as the sky in your images may be darker on one side than the other: the effect can look very odd. This can be corrected in Photoshop, but it's tricky. You should also note that glare will only be removed from non-metallic surfaces such as paintwork, foliage and plastic. To remove reflections from surfaces such as water and glass, the angle between the reflective surface and the lens axis must be around 30°. You can find this by making slight adjustments to your position then rotating the polariser to see what happens.

Finally, polarising filters can give your pictures a slight blue colour cast when used in bright, sunny weather. To remove this, either adjust your camera's White Balance setting or correct the cast when you process the Raw file on your computer.

No filter

With polariser

Beef up your blue sky and add visual impact to scenics by using a polarising filter.

Neutral Density (ND)

Lengthen exposure times for creative effects using a Neutral Density filter

ND FILTERS ARE specially made to reduce the amount of light entering your lens without changing the colour balance – hence the name Neutral Density. They do a similar job to ND grad filters, but instead of affecting just part of the image (usually the sky with ND grads), they have a uniform effect on the whole image.

ND filters are mainly used to increase the exposure required for an image, so you can use a slower shutter speed to record motion. The classic subject where they're used is waterfalls to record the moving water as a graceful blur. But they can be used to introduce or increase motion in all kinds of subjects – crowds of commuters pouring off a train, traffic moving along busy roads, trees blowing in the wind, waves washing over rocks and so on. They're ideal for use in very bright conditions when the lowest ISO rating and smallest aperture aren't enough to give you the slow shutter speed you desire.

Exposure chart

If you're using weaker ND filters, up to a 1.2 density, your camera's TTL metering will be able to give accurate exposure readings with the filter on the lens. Once density goes beyond 1.2, however, you may find that underexposure occurs because the filter density fools the camera's metering. To avoid exposure error, take a meter reading without the ND filter on the lens then calculate the required exposure with it in place and set the exposure on your camera manually. If you have an iPhone there's a useful app called ND Calc that will do this for you. Alternatively, refer to the table below. Once the required exposure goes beyond 30 seconds you will have to set your camera to Bulb (B) mode and time the exposure using the timer on the camera or Smartphone, a remote release, your wristwatch or by counting elephants!

Unfiltered	With 0.6ND	With 0.9ND	With 1.2ND
1/500sec	1/125sec	1/60sec	1/30sec
1/250sec	1/60sec	1/30sec	1/15sec
1/125sec	1/30sec	1/15sec	1/8sec
1/60sec	1/15sec	1/8sec	1/4sec
1/30sec	1/8sec	1/4sec	1/2sec
1/15sec	1/4sec	1/2sec	1sec
1/8sec	1/2sec	1sec	2secs
1/4sec	1sec	2secs	4secs
1/2sec	2secs	4secs	8secs
1sec	4secs	8secs	16secs
2secs	8secs	16secs	32secs
3secs	16secs	32secs	1min
4sec	32secs	1min	2mins

Technique watch!

Different densities

The amount of exposure increase an ND filter requires depends on its density. The weakest ND worth bothering with is a 0.6 (4x), which requires a two-stop exposure increase. A polariser also requires an exposure increase of two stops and so can be used like a 0.6ND filter. Next up is a 0.9 (8x), which requires a three-stop exposure increase, followed by a 1.2 (16x) which requires a four-stop increase. This is where the density of conventional ND filters end, though you can combine two or more for a cumulative effect – 0.6 and 0.9NDs together will require a five-stop exposure increase, for example.

The alternative is to use a more extreme ND filter, with a density of 1.8 (six stops) or more. These filters were originally designed for photographing industrial processes that involved extreme brightness but are now popular with photographers as they allow exposures in daylight of several minutes. Turn over for our favourite: the 3.0ND, which requires an exposure increase of ten stops – that's 1000x more than the unfiltered exposure!

No filter

0.6ND

Using an **ND** filter allows you to use longer shutter speeds in daylight: ideal when shooting waterfalls.

1.2ND

3.0ND

Colour casts

While ND filters should be neutral, once you combine them for higher density (and a longer exposure), you'll see that colour casts appear. This is most noticeable with ten-stop ND filters – the B+W 3.0 adds a very warm colour cast while the Lee Big Stopper adds a cool blue cast. These can enhance the look of the image, but if you prefer, you can adjust the colour temperature when you process the Raw file.

Ten-stop ND

Use a ten-stop ND filter and you'll find you can create colour and black & white fine-art landscapes with ease

THE FIRST THING you'll notice when using a ten-stop ND filter is that it's so dense, you can't see through it. In bright sunlight you might just make out a faint image through the viewfinder, but its brightness is 1000x less than if you didn't have the ten-stop ND in place. To take a photograph you must therefore mount your camera on a tripod, compose the scene, set focus to manual (as AF won't work through it), align your ND grad in its holder if you're using one, then finally position the ten-stop ND. Some of the latest cameras have LiveView that's sensitive enough to see through a ten-stop ND, so if you need to adjust the composition or move the camera and shoot from a different spot, you may be able to do so without removing the ten-stop ND filter. For most of us, though, removing the filter to see through the viewfinder is unavoidable. That's why Lee Filter's slot-in Big Stopper is more versatile than the B+W screw-in filter – you can simply remove the Big Stopper from its holder and leave everything else in place, whereas the B+W has to be unscrewed from the lens.

The longest exposure you can achieve using your camera's programmed shutter speed range is 30 seconds, but more often than not you'll be using exposures much longer than that with the ten-stopper, so you'll need to set your camera to Bulb (B) mode in order to keep the shutter open. Trying to keep exposures under 30 seconds for convenience, by opening up the aperture or increasing the ISO rating, is defeating the object because you'll get the best effects by using exposures of several minutes.

In terms of subject matter, any scene containing moving elements is ideal. The sky is an obvious candidate: on a windy day, clouds are transformed into ghostly streaks as they drift overhead, and you won't know quite how they're going to record until the exposure ends and you can review the shot. Trees and grass swaying in the breeze also take on a totally different appearance when exposed for several minutes, adding a strong sense of motion to an image.

Coastal scenes are perhaps the most effective subjects for the ten-stop ND. The sea is constantly moving, so over the course of a few minutes any texture in its surface is lost and it takes on a smooth, milky appearance that contrasts well with static elements such as piers, lighthouses, headlands, jetties and rocks. Or for something completely different, try shooting urban scenes with a ten-stop ND. Anything moving through the scene while the shutter is open – people and traffic mostly – won't record. This means you can capture something that we never see with the naked eye – busy streets completely deserted!

Wide-angle lenses are more effective than telephotos when using a ten-stop ND because you can emphasise the sky and the foreground, which is where most of the motion is recorded. Move in close to a static feature in the foreground and contrast it with moving water, or get down

1/4sec with no filter

4mins with ten-stop ND

low with a wide lens so you're looking up at the sky.

Bright sunshine gives the least effective light for ten-stop shots as it's harsh and flat, plus the higher light levels mean you won't be able to achieve really long exposures even with your lens stopped right down and the ISO at its minimum setting. Dawn and dusk are perfect for atmospheric images, along with early morning and evening when the sun's low in the sky and the light is nice and warm. The B+W 3.0 ten-stop ND has a warm colour cast, which is ideal for enhancing shots taken at either end of the day. Stormy weather produces dramatic results as there's more movement in the sky and sea, while on overcast days the soft light and gentle tones result in simple, graphic images.

Although you'll be shooting in colour, ten-stop shots look amazing in black & white, so be prepared to experiment. Treat the sky and the rest of the scene as separate elements and apply Levels and Curves to both to really bring out the drama and contrast in the image. The end result may look nothing like the original scene, but that doesn't matter because as soon as you put a ten-stop ND filter on your lens, you're taking a step back from reality anyway.

Exposure chart

The chart on the right reveals the increase of exposure times when using a ten-stop ND filter. It's a key reason why you're recommended not to use the Long Exposure Noise Reduction system on your camera, as this function takes the same amount of time as the exposure. So shoot a two-minute exposure and you'll need to wait a couple more for the image to write. We'd suggest you switch Noise Reduction off and control noise in post-production.

Unfiltered	3.0ND (Ten-stop)
1/500sec	Two seconds
1/250sec	Four seconds
1/125sec	Eight seconds
1/60sec	16 seconds
1/30sec	32 seconds
1/15sec	One minute
1/8sec	Two minutes
1/4sec	Four minutes
1/2sec	Eight minutes
One second	16 minutes
Two seconds	32 minutes
Three seconds	48 minutes
Four seconds	One hour

The ten-stop ND is the filter of the moment. Don't leave home without one.

ND grads & Photoshop

A Neutral Density grad darkens skies for a more balanced image, but Mark Bauer explains how post-processing can be needed for certain scenes

ONE OF THE MAIN technical challenges in landscape photography is controlling the contrast in a scene so that you can accurately record detail in both the land and the sky. Often the sky is a lot brighter than the land, and the contrast is beyond what the camera's sensor can record, resulting in either a well-exposed sky and underexposed foreground, or the opposite. A way around this is to use a Neutral Density (ND) graduated filter. As previously mentioned, these filters are brilliantly simple – they are dark at the top and clear at the bottom and all you do is position the dark half over the brighter area of the picture, reducing contrast between the light and dark areas thus enabling you to capture detail in both the foreground and the sky. The only problem is that the dividing line between the dark and light areas of an ND grad is a straight line, and not all landscapes have a straight horizon – often the horizon is broken by an object such as a tree, a hill or a building, and the filter can cause an unnatural-looking darkening of the top of these objects. However, help is at hand as, most of the time, post-processing will rescue the shot. Here I explain how to use an ND grad and remove its effect from specific areas.

1 Arriving at Portland in Dorset just before dawn, I took a spot meter reading from the foreground rocks and the sky, which revealed a difference in brightness of around four stops. Although this falls within the dynamic range of the sensor, shadow detail has been compromised a little, and lifting this in post-processing could reveal noise in the image.

2 With a four-stop difference between the rocks and the sky, I chose a three-stop ND grad filter, as it would leave the sky a little bit lighter than the foreground. The next choice was to use a soft or hard grad (see panel). Soft grads aren't always the best choice for seascapes, as the brightest part of the scene is often across the horizon line, so I decided on a hard grad.

3 Using the hard grad filter has resulted in a much more even exposure, but there is a problem. The top half of the lighthouse, where the filter has cut into it, is a bit too dark. The effect is fairly subtle, but it's definitely there, and doesn't look natural. Fortunately, this common problem can be easily sorted out with a spot of post-processing work.

Hard and soft grad filters

Neutral Density graduated filters come in two varieties: hard and soft. Hard grads have a very obvious and sudden transition from the dark to clear areas, whereas soft grads have a much more gradual transition. Hard grads are more useful in situations where the horizon line is fairly straight and doesn't have any large objects breaking it. Soft grads on the other hand are a better option when you have an uneven horizon.

Also, opt for a hard grad if you intend to shoot a scene with a straight horizon at sunset or sunrise, as the horizon line will be the brightest part of the scene, and soft grads won't hold back enough light.

When you're shooting a scene at sunrise/sunset, which has a large object such as a tree or building breaking the horizon, a combination of filter and Photoshop is the best bet.

Final image

This is the final result, exhibiting good detail and colour in the sky and foreground, and a natural-looking lighthouse without a darker section at the top.

4 Using the *Magnetic Lasso Tool* in Photoshop, I selected the darker top half of the lighthouse, so that I could work on the problem area without affecting any other part of the image. I decided not to apply any feathering to the selection, as this could leave a 'halo' around the lighthouse once I'd finished lightening the selection.

5 There are various ways of lightening or darkening images, such as *Curves* and *Levels*, but for this selection I use the *Dodge Tool*, as I could paint the effect on gradually and build it up in the areas that needed it more. I set the *Exposure* value to 10%, which enabled me to work gradually on lightening the selection.

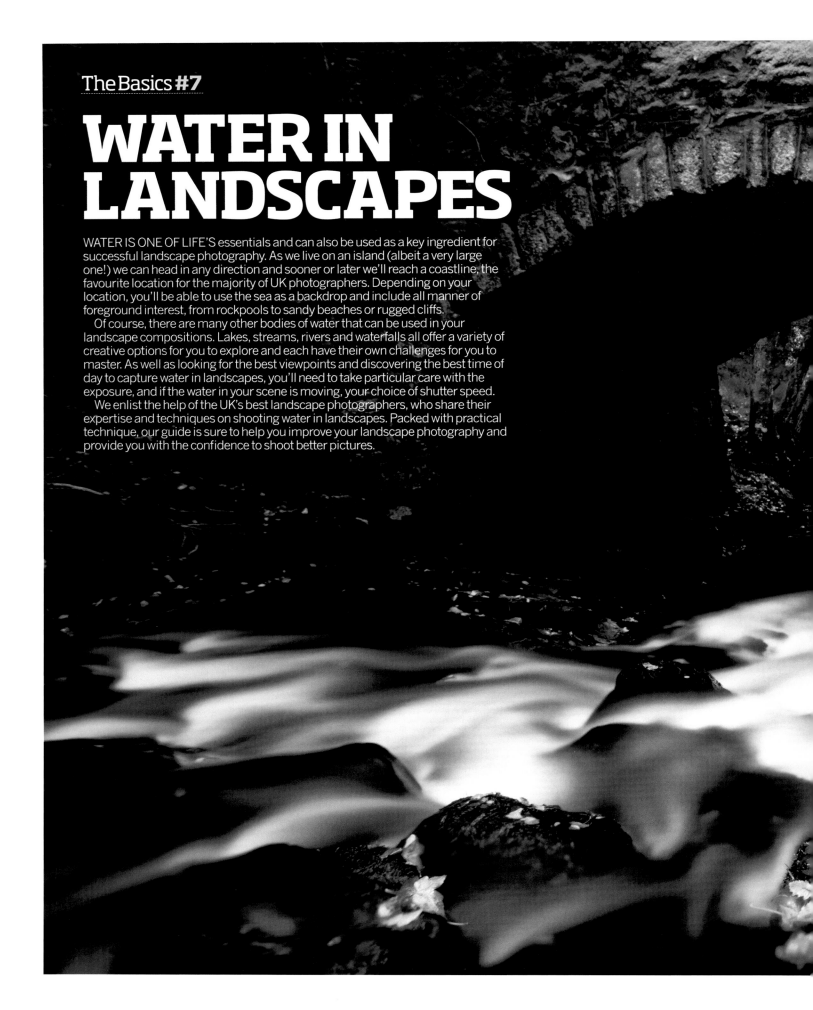

WATER IN LANDSCAPES

WATER IS ONE OF LIFE'S essentials and can also be used as a key ingredient for successful landscape photography. As we live on an island (albeit a very large one!) we can head in any direction and sooner or later we'll reach a coastline; the favourite location for the majority of UK photographers. Depending on your location, you'll be able to use the sea as a backdrop and include all manner of foreground interest, from rockpools to sandy beaches or rugged cliffs.

Of course, there are many other bodies of water that can be used in your landscape compositions. Lakes, streams, rivers and waterfalls all offer a variety of creative options for you to explore and each have their own challenges for you to master. As well as looking for the best viewpoints and discovering the best time of day to capture water in landscapes, you'll need to take particular care with the exposure, and if the water in your scene is moving, your choice of shutter speed.

We enlist the help of the UK's best landscape photographers, who share their expertise and techniques on shooting water in landscapes. Packed with practical technique, our guide is sure to help you improve your landscape photography and provide you with the confidence to shoot better pictures.

The basics for shooting water in landscapes

Get prepared to head out in to the great outdoors to shoot stunning scenery by ensuring you have the best techniques and the right gear

WE'RE NOT SURE if you've ever noticed, but the majority of stunning landscape images usually has some form of water in the scene. Whether it's as subtle as a small trickling river, or as obvious as a dominating sea in a coastal seascape, water represents a key element in many landscape images.

One of the main reasons for this is because water is a photographically pliable element. By using filters and/or manipulating the shutter speed, it's possible to record water in all manner of ways, from freezing its movement so droplets are suspended in mid-air, to using a long exposure to transform it into an ethereal mist. While potentially causing problems with our exposure, the reflective nature of water

also plays its part in improving images too. On days where there is little or no wind, by heading to a lake, reservoir or any other large body of water, it's possible to produce a striking result by capturing a clean reflection of the scene on its surface. The possibilities don't stop there – rivers can be used as strong lead-in lines through the scene or, along with the likes of secluded rockpools and meandering streams littered with rocks, can form highly effective foreground interest.

The list is endless, but in this section, we provide the essentials you need to start going out to shoot water in landscapes and returning with brilliant results. What are you waiting for, keep on reading and get exploring!

Choosing shutter speeds

The shutter speed you use to capture water depends on a number of factors: how quickly it's moving, how much of it there is and whether you want to stop it dead or let it blur. For big waterfalls and breaking waves, a shutter speed of 1/1000-1/2000sec will guarantee you freeze every droplet. For fast-flowing rivers and smaller waterfalls like the one here, try 1/200–1/500sec, while for slower rivers and streams 1/125–1/250sec should do the trick. When it comes to blurring, one second will have a good effect on big waterfalls or try two seconds for smaller waterfalls. Rivers and streams need a slower speed of two to four seconds, though you can go much slower – 10-20 seconds – if you like. Overexposure can be a problem when large volumes of water are concentrated in certain areas, so keep an eye on the histogram and use a faster speed if you start to clip the highlights. For coastal scenes, one to two seconds will blur waves, while 20-30 seconds will produce a 'milky' effect.

1/60sec

1/20sec

0.4 seconds

Shoot water the way you ought to!

Dramatic coastlines are the perfect place to put theory into practice when it comes to photographing scenes with water. Follow our advice on the gear to use, the techniques to try and the settings to make and you'll soon be taking landscape images like a pro.

IMAGE: HELEN DIXON

Water and composition

You won't have to travel far to find water. In hilly regions, waterfalls are relatively common, whilst rivers and streams meander through our countryside. In towns and cities, waterways and canals are a common sight and large bodies of water, like lakes, lochs and reservoirs, are dotted around all over the country.

In the UK, you are never that far from the coast and the sea provides photographers with a huge number of opportunities. It creates the perfect backdrop to sandy or rocky bays and rugged cliffs. Whilst the sea is photogenic on calm days, it is at its most dramatic in rough, stormy weather when large, crashing waves bring energy and movement to coastal landscapes. A river, winding its way through your composition, will guide the eye through the image – effectively increasing the photo's depth and interest. Streams and rivers are perfect subjects to create an 'S' curve or lead-in line. Small puddles can also help composition, creating ideal foreground interest. For example, the shallow pools exposed at low-tide are very photogenic. They will help to add a three-dimensional feel to your pictures if you attach a wide-angle lens and photograph them from nearby to emphasise their curves and reflections.

Water works well when photographed as the main subject. A wide-angle lens, such as an 11-22mm, together with a low viewpoint close to the surface of a river, will create the impression that the water is practically flowing into the camera – but only do this if it's completely safe. To ensure maximum sharpness, ensure sufficient depth-of-field by choosing a small aperture, such as f/13-16, and focus one-third of the way into the scene, using the LCD monitor to check the result.

MOTION SLICKNESS
By leaving the shutter open for a long exposure, moving water becomes a mist that is spread across the scene at the average height of the waves and ripples. Flowing bubbles (right) form streaks that follow the stream. The longer the exposure, the less defined the waves become.

Reflections in water

On calm, still days the surface of any body of water will act like a mirror, perfectly reflecting its surroundings and the sky above. Reflections are a favourite subject among landscape photographers, particularly on large bodies of water when strong colours are also evident – during sunrise or sunset, for instance.

Rocks jutting out of the water, tall reeds, a jetty or rowing boats are among the objects that work well as part of a reflected landscape, adding scale and context to the image. The rule-of-thirds states that landscape photographers shouldn't place the horizon centrally in the frame. However, when photographing reflections of a reservoir or loch, a centred horizon will often create a symmetrical result and actually strengthen composition.

Be careful if you are using a polarising filter to saturate colour and deepen blue skies. A polariser can also reduce the intensity of reflections – although to what degree will depend on the camera angle in relation to the reflected surface. In some situations, you may have to decide what is of higher priority – a deep blue sky and saturated colours, but poor reflections; or strong, vivid reflections, but sky and colours that are weaker. A polariser can actually intensify reflections by removing the sheen from the water's surface. Therefore, continue using a polariser, just carefully regulate its effect on the reflections within the scene, by peering through the camera's viewfinder as you rotate the filter in its mount.

If there are distracting ripples on the water, consider using a solid ND filter to lengthen exposure time. A shutter speed exceeding a second will help to eliminate gentle ripples and help maximise the strength of the reflections.

ON REFLECTION
These two images featuring reflections in water show how applying the rule-of-thirds (left) and ignoring it (right) both have their place. As the shot of the mountain lake demonstrates, running the far shoreline across the middle of the frame creates a powerful symmetry. Don't be tempted to skim stones!

Water and exposure

Moving water has a tendency to appear white. As a result, accurate exposure is essential – overexposure will lead to white water being 'burnt out' and devoid of detail. Even if you shoot in Raw, such detail cannot be retrieved during post-processing, which is why it is important to achieve the correct exposure at the time of capture.

Your camera's multi-zone meter can normally be relied upon to achieve the right exposure. However, don't rely on the replayed image on your DSLR's LCD monitor to assess exposure. Instead, view the image's histogram. The graph represents the distribution of tones within the scene. Far left (0) represents pure black; far right (255) pure white; whilst the middle area covers mid-tones. If water is overexposed, this will be indicated by sharp peaks to the far right of the graph.

Most DSLRs also have a 'highlights' screen. This alert causes groups of pixels that have exceeded the sensor's dynamic range to flash as a warning. If water within your landscape is overexposed, apply negative exposure compensation. Problems occur in very bright daylight – particularly around midday. Brightly lit, frothy white water can prove very intense and there is no simple way to achieve an overall correct exposure in-camera. This is why the softer, less intense light of early morning and evening is better suited to shooting water.

The quality of light on overcast days is also excellent for shooting water, particularly if using long exposure to blur its movement. So, if it is a dull day, don't stay indoors – head to your nearest river or coast instead and start shooting!

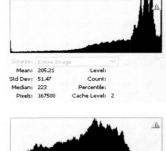

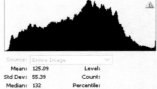

REVIEW YOUR HISTOGRAM
These two histograms show the difference between an overexposed scene and one that has been exposed correctly. The top diagram, showing all the peaks to the far right of the horizontal scale and crashing the top of the vertical scale, indicates 'clipping' or overexposure. The highlights have exceeded the ability of the sensor to retain image information and this data is lost forever. Post-processing in Photoshop will not be able to get it back. Look for a more even spread of peaks, without clipping, as shown in the second histogram.

Water movement – freeze or blur?

How best to capture water's motion is a contentious issue. Some photographers like to capture water authentically, freezing its movement using a fast shutter speed. Others prefer to intentionally blur it in order to create the feeling of motion. Both techniques work well in the right situation. However, it is important to do one or the other – somewhere in between, when the water is neither blurred or sharp, will usually just look messy and unintentional.

If you wish to suspend water movement, you'll usually need to employ a shutter speed of 1/500sec or faster – although the exact speed required will depend on the speed of the water. Landscape photographers normally use a small aperture (large f/number) to achieve a depth-of-field big enough to render both foreground and background detail in sharp focus. As a result, they are often working with slow exposures, especially when light levels are low.

This is one reason why many photographers go to the other extreme, employing a lengthy exposure to blur the water's flow. To many eyes, this 'blurred' effect, creates more pleasing results – adding life and movement to images. An exposure of 0.5sec should do the job, but a speed of several seconds is preferable – this is guaranteed to create an attractive silky, white blur. In order to generate a long exposure, employ the lens's minimum aperture (typically f/22) and ensure that the camera's lowest ISO setting is selected. If the resulting shutter speed still isn't sufficiently slow, you'll need to use a filter.

Neutral density (ND) filters are designed to block light entering the camera – basically, they alter the light's brightness, but not its colour. They allow photographers to employ artificially long exposures in order to blur subject movement. They are available in different strengths – commonly 1-, 2- and 3-stop densities – and as both screw- and slot-in types. A two-stop version will normally be sufficient. Your camera's TTL metering will automatically adjust for the density.

USE AN ND FILTER
Sometimes you might have to reduce the amount of light coming into the lens to force down shutter speeds and create the blur. Neutral Density (ND) filters will do the trick. Polarising filters also reduce the light level by two stops, facilitating slow shutter speeds, but watch out for the effect on reflections.

1/1000sec

1/2sec

Capturing 'natural-looking' waves

Professional photographer Mark Bauer explains the best technique for capturing the movement of breaking waves as they hit the shore

There's a lot of debate about how best to photograph wave movement. Long exposures result in a 'misty' look that is popular with many photographers (see over the page) but is certainly not to everyone's taste as it's not authentic. When we watch waves rolling on to the shore, we see the whole movement – we don't see a moment frozen in time or mist drifting over rocks. One way to truly appreciate wave motion as the eye sees it is to use video rather than a stills camera, but by paying careful attention to shutter speeds, it is possible to record natural-looking waves in your images.

The trick is to record the right amount of movement; if the shutter is open too long there will be too much motion blur, not long enough and the wave will appear too static. You need to find a middle ground where there's misty blur but the waves still keep their shape.

There is no simple recipe for this; the best shutter speed depends on the size and speed of the waves, how they're falling onto the shore, and also personal taste. Experimentation is the key – be prepared to shoot a lot of frames and spend a lot of time looking at the review screen and tweaking the camera controls.

Controlling shutter speeds

Although there's no 'ideal' shutter speed for capturing a breaking wave, as it depends on the conditions at the time, a shutter speed of between ¼ second and a couple of seconds usually provides the result you'll want.

It's not just a matter, however, of putting the camera into shutter-priority mode and setting the shutter speed. You will also need to make sure you're using the right aperture in order to achieve the appropriate depth-of-field and an accurate exposure. For landscapes this is usually between f/8 and f/22 for maximum depth-of-field.

There are other ways you can control the shutter speed too. Apart from waiting for the light to change, for a faster shutter speed, you should increase the camera's ISO rating. Normally this will raise the level of noise, so you do not want to go much above ISO 800 unless you're using a professional DSLR that handles noise well.

For shutter speeds of more than 30 seconds, you will need to set your camera to Bulb mode and time the exposure manually. However this can often result in overexposed shots, so you may need to add a solid Neutral Density filter to reduce the amount of light falling onto the sensor. ND filters come in various strengths, the most common being one, two and three stops and you can use several together, along with a polarising filter too, for extremely long exposures.

1 I compose the scene so that the waves are falling onto the foreground rocks and then check the exposure for the sky and ground separately using my DSLR's spot meter.

2 As the sky is much brighter than the ground, I add a three-stop **ND** soft grad filter to balance the contrast. A soft grad means the transition line won't be too obvious.

3 Set to shutter-priority mode, I try 1/100sec but it freezes the movement. For large waves this might convey drama, but with small waves like this it completely fails.

4 In the hope of lengthening the exposure, I wait for the light levels to drop and replace the three-stop ND filter with a four-stop ND filter, giving me a ten-second exposure at f/22.

5 This time the exposure is still not long enough to give an ethereal misty look to the water, but it doesn't capture the drama of the scene by freezing the water either.

6 Opening up the aperture to f/11, and swapping the four-stop ND for a two-stop enables me to shorten the exposure time to 0.3 seconds. The result is almost what I wanted, but the wave is frozen just a little too much.

7 One more attempt, now the light levels are a bit lower, and I get the shot I want at around 0.6 of a second. There's enough movement to create a sense of drama but the waves still keeps their shape.

Final image
Opening up the aperture to f/11 allows me to set a shutter speed of half a second, while still retaining plenty of depth-of-field. The result creates drama and avoids the waves looking like mist. I particularly like the way the spray is rising over the rocks in the middle distance.

Create misty-looking waterscapes

Pro photographer Ross Hoddinott leads the way to capturing ethereal images of moving water

WHEN YOU LIVE on an island the size of the UK, the coast is never far away, which is handy considering few subjects are as popular as seascapes for shooting. How you capture the water's motion, however, can make or break your photographs. While some loathe the blurry water effect, most love it. The most striking results are when you can get close to the action and where the water 'shapes' your foreground rocks as it washes over them, but getting this depends on the tide. Opt for a receding tide as it's safer to photograph, but always be mindful of large waves and put your safety above 'getting the shot'. A winter's evening is perfect for capturing long exposure landscapes as the light is naturally soft and low. With this in mind, I visited Trebarwith Strand in North Cornwall with the sole intention of shooting moving water. I arrived an hour before sunset armed with a range of filters to help me achieve the dreamy, angel-mist water I desired.

Kit watch!

◼ Tripod

To photograph moving water, a good, sturdy tripod is essential. A camera support will ensure that everything other than the water remains pin-sharp. Also, if you want to avoid wet feet, wellies are a good idea.

1 CHOOSE YOUR VIEWPOINT There is no point going to great lengths to attractively blur the water if your composition is poor. In this instance, I looked for a rocky outcrop that would form a strong foreground and lead the eye into the image. Try to imagine how the water's motion will shape the foreground when it is blurred. A vertical composition will often help create depth in a shot.

2 TAKE A TEST SHOT In aperture-priority mode, select f/16 for sufficient depth-of-field and ISO 100 to generate a long exposure. Avoid stopping down as far as f/22, as diffraction (softening of the image) can affect results. For me, this resulted in a shutter speed of ¼sec, which created a degree of subject motion but not as much as I wanted. It's time to artificially lengthen the exposure.

3 ADD FILTERS A stop is a doubling or halving of the exposure value. Therefore, an ND filter with a three-stop density (0.9ND) lengthens an unfiltered value of ¼sec to two seconds – a significant shift. In low light, and when using high density ND filters, TTL metering is more prone to error – particularly underexposure. Remember to regularly review images and histograms.

4 AND WAIT... With the ND filter, the motion looked far more attractive, but for a real ethereal-looking result, I simply waited for the sun to lower, lengthening the shutter speed.

Exposure settings

Mode: Aperture-priority
Metering: Multi-zone
Exposure: One minute at f/16 (ISO 100)

Final image

Fifteen minutes later, with the sun having set, the shutter speed was lengthened to a minute, and I was able to achieve this dreamy result.

Shoot moving water

Lee Frost reveals how the correct shutter speed is essential when scenes include running water

ALTHOUGH IT HAS become something of a cliché, using a slow shutter speed to record moving water as a graceful, milky blur is an undeniably effective technique, which is why so many photographers, including myself, like to use it. From tumbling mountain streams to bubbling brooks and thundering waterfalls, wherever you find moving water, the same basic approach can be used to capture it and turn an ordinary scene into a creative image that's full of atmosphere. Even better, moving water is best shot on an overcast day with soft light so there are no blinding highlights to contend with, caused by sunlight reflecting on the water. This makes it a perfect subject for those dull, grey days photographers in the UK know so well!

TECHNIQUE WATCH!

■ **Select a slow shutter speed**
When shooting moving water, you need to use a shutter speed that's slow enough to blur the water, so it records smooth, but not too slow that areas where the water is more concentrated start to overexpose and burn out. This is a matter of trial and error, but an exposure of one second usually makes a good starting point. The great thing about digital capture is that you can check each shot you take to see how it looks, then shorten or lengthen the exposure time until you get the perfect result.

If tiny areas of water burn out, don't worry – when you download the images and view them as full-size files, chances are those highlight warnings will have disappeared. And if they haven't, it's a simple job to use the Clone Stamp Tool in Photoshop to copy and paste water from a different part of the image over the overexposed areas.

1 Because a slow shutter speed is used to blur the water's movement, you should always mount your camera on a sturdy tripod to keep it steady. It's also a good idea to attach a remote release so you can trip the shutter without touching the camera, which risks vibrations that could lead to your images being ruined by shake.

2 In dull weather, stopping your lens down to f/16 or f/22 and setting a low ISO may give you a shutter speed slow enough to blur the water. If not, use a Neutral Density (ND) filter to increase the exposure. A polarising filter can also be used to increase the exposure by two stops – so 1/4sec becomes one second, for example.

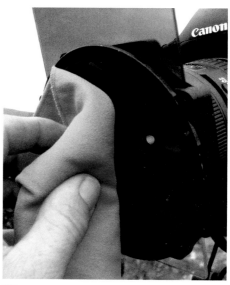

3 Before taking a shot, check the lens or filter for water droplets. If you're shooting close to a waterfall splashes or spray may get on the lens. I n this case, drizzle was the culprit. Wipe the water away with a clean microfibre cloth otherwise image quality will suffer. Holding an umbrella over the camera can help in rainy weather.

4 Take your first shot and review it. I was initially attracted to this spout of water hitting a rock and cascading in all directions. Shooting side-on proved to be a good angle and a shutter speed of one second provided enough blur. The shot worked, but there were many other options to explore.

5 I decided to try a wider view, using the water spout in the previous step as foreground interest, carrying the eye up the ravine towards the distant peaks of the Cuillin Ridge. It took a few attempts to get the shutter speed just right so no areas of the moving water were overexposed.

Final image

Here's the end result, shot with an exposure of 1.3 seconds at f/22 (ISO 50), using a 0.9ND filter to increase the exposure and a 0.6ND hard graduate to hold detail in the sky. The dull weather and soft light worked well, perfectly revealing the subtle colours in the scene, while the blurred water captures the feel of the tumbling mountain stream.

Learn to shoot dramatic lighthouse scenes

Lighthouses are a favourite focal point for coastal landscapes – here's how to make the most of them

WHEN YOU LIVE in a country surrounded by water, you are never too far away from a lighthouse. Designed to aid navigation and mark hazardous coastline, the number of operational lighthouses in the UK especially has declined. However, there is still around 70 fully-functional lighthouses, managed by Trinity House, and there are countries where lighthouses remain a staple of their coastline.

Traditional lighthouses are so appealing: they're romantic, often remote and located in wild, unforgiving environments. They are also highly photogenic, either in frame-filling close-up, or as part of a wider view to show them in context with their coastal surroundings. If you are unsure where the closest lighthouse is, do research online. If you're in the UK try www.trinityhouse.co.uk.

Accessibility is the first consideration when shooting lighthouses as they can be remote and involve a steep walk to a suitable viewpoint. Always put safety first: don't venture close to the cliff edge or far from recognised paths. Typically, the best time to photograph lighthouses is at dawn or dusk. At dusk, working lighthouses are operational, which combined with a twilight sky, can create very evocative images. With low light comes long exposures, so there's no need for a solid ND filter to creatively blur water and cloud movement, but you will need a tripod!

To maximise image quality, select a low ISO and opt for an mid-aperture (f/11 or f/16) if you have foreground interest and need lots of depth-of-field. Your camera's TTL metering is likely to be fooled in low light, so check histograms to ensure the correct exposure. If shutter speed exceeds 30 seconds, you'll need to switch to Bulb mode, hold the shutter open manually using a remote release, and time the exposure with a watch. Your window of opportunity will be short, though. As it gets darker, the intensity of the light beam increases, so the image is likely to overexpose, with the lantern's intensity burning out important detail. Try placing your hand, or piece of black card, in front of the lens for the split-second it takes for the beam to sweep over your location. Thanks to the length of exposure and the short time you shield the lens, this process will not be visible in the final image.

Bad weather can also create dramatic results. Dark, menacing clouds emphasise the exposed nature and role of the building. Although the trend is to blur the motion of the sea using a long exposure, try capturing crashing waves authentically with a fast exposure for spectacular results. Timing is important: release the shutter just as a wave crashes against the land. Don't be afraid to take a series of images to capture a perfectly timed result. Finally, beware of spray. Even if you shoot from the clifftops, spray can degrade image quality. Keep a lens cloth handy and shield the front of the lens between frames. When you return home, give the camera a wipe down with a damp cloth to clear any salt residue.

TECHNIQUE WATCH

■ Composition

Composition is key to lighthouse photography. Focal length will be a major contributing factor to how you compose the scene: by selecting a longer or shorter focal length, you can radically alter the look and feel of the final result. A short focal length – say, 17-35mm – will show the building in context with its environment, creating a sense of scale and size. To emphasise the remoteness of the location, include plenty of negative space. The most stimulating composition typically results from placing the building on a dividing third. But placing the lighthouse centrally can also work, especially with a square crop. Wider views allow you to include interesting skies, seas, and the shape and ruggedness of the coastline. Longer focal lengths will isolate detail and the shape and colour of the lighthouse itself. The long end of a 70-300mm telezoom is perfect for this. Alternatively, if you can get physically close to the lighthouse, get closer and shoot it using a wide-angle lens. A low-perspective, looking up, will create distortion, highlighting the building's sheer height and size for a striking composition.

21mm

70mm

Kit watch!

■ Essential equipment

✔ Lenses covering a range of focal lengths – a wide-angle zoom and telezoom are ideal

✔ A solid ND filter for creatively blurring water and cloud movement

✔ A torch to safely guide you to and from the car in semi-darkness

✔ A stable tripod and a remote release

✔ Lens cloths, to remove sea spray

✔ A piece of black card, should you wish to shield the lens from the beam of the lantern

1) Capturing the rich colour and atmosphere of a sunset can add vital interest to your image. Use an exposure of a few seconds to blur movement.

2) Find the best viewpoint. A clifftop view can make a striking vantage point, but remember to put your safety first!

3) Paths make strong lead-in lines, especially if placed centrally in the frame as they lead the eye towards the focal point.

4) A striking silhouette can look incredibly dramatic so make sure to visit lighthouses at dusk. Take a spot reading from a mid-tone and regularly check the histogram on your monitor.

5) Pick a quick exposure to capture the action of waves crashing against the rocks.

6) Extend your exposures by using ND filters to achieve ethereal shots like this.

REXTON

Robust, stable, water-resistant, comfortable to carry and full of thought-out details

This is what makes the Rexton Camera bag series a reliable outdoor companion for everyone! With our 10 year guarantee on all Rexton models, this is a series you can continuously count on to protect your equipment while you are on the move.

Imaging

Entertainment

Computer

Mobile

Gaming

Sat Nav

Home & Living

The smart solution

The Basics **#8**

UNDERSTANDING COLOUR

A LOT OF TIME, energy and thought has been devoted to the study of colour, its practical applications and its psychological effects. Often those applications and effects are linked. It's not an accident that stop signs are red, cool settings on air conditioning are blue or that the environmental movement has adopted the colour green.

Much can be learned about the relationships between colours, too. Colours work together in different ways, with certain combinations creating energy and tension, while others harmonise and create calm. When a colour appears in nature with a greater than normal intensity, the stage is set for great landscape photography. Learning their relationship will reap rewards.

1) Harmony and contrast

There are basically two types of relationship between colours – harmony and contrast. Looking at a colour wheel helps us to understand this. Colours that are next to each other, for example blue and green, are harmonious, while those that are opposite, for example blue and yellow, contrast with each other.

Also, colours that are on the 'warm' side of the wheel harmonise with each other, while all those on the 'cool' side also harmonise. Harmonious colours are more calming to look at, and blues and greens in particular are very tranquil. Contrasting colours are more dramatic and create a tension that can challenge the eye – blue and yellow is a strong contrast.

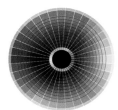

THE COLOUR WHEEL
Contrasting colours such as yellow and blue, or red and green create tension and drama. Colours adjacent to each other are calming.

ADAM BURTON

2) Colour and emotion

As well as having visual impact, colours can suggest different moods, evoke different emotions and can have symbolic significance related to our culture and background. Think about the effect a dominant colour might have on your image. It might be appropriate to subdue a colour, or emphasise it. Consider colour in the composition, the lighting and through careful use of filtration.

RED is an intense colour, especially when contrasted against a dark background. It is a colour universally used for warning or danger and is hard to ignore. Red is the most powerful and attention-grabbing colour in photography, though it can prove distracting if included small within the landscape, for instance, a distant car, boat or letterbox.

BLUE is a retiring colour, which can be employed to convey restfulness, sadness or tranquility. In photography, it is commonly used to convey coldness, which works especially well when combined with water and wintry scenes. Blue is a very important colour for landscape photographers as a saturated sky creates a flattering backdrop.

GREEN is often used to signify health and life. Obviously, green is the predominant colour of vegetation and therefore it is dominant in many scenic images. Green is easily overwhelmed by bright advancing colours like red and, generally speaking, has less impact. However, when isolated, green can still create strong, interesting images.

YELLOW is another bold, advancing colour, often used to represent happiness or brightness. It will add warmth to your image and works particularly well when combined or contrasted with blue. Yellow, along with similarly rich colours, like gold and orange, epitomise autumn. It can prove a good background for still-life images.

3) Using only one colour

Single colours often give an image a particular mood and it's possible to make successful compositions using just one colour – or shades of one colour.

Certain lighting conditions can create this effect and add atmosphere to a scene. An intensely orange or red sunset will give every neutral colour a strong bias, bathing a scene in a fiery warmth.

Also, strong backlighting can desaturate colours, creating an almost monochromatic effect; while at pre-sunrise and post-sunset, there is no single strong light source and the light is diffused and reflected down from the sky.

The two images on the right are really good examples of monochromatic images. Starting over on the far right you can see how backlighting has drained the colours from this scene, resulting in an image that appears almost devoid of colour.

The predawn light bathing the lake and dead wood in the near-right picture is diffused, falling on the scene from virtually the whole sky. It has given the scene a fairly cold cast, but the mood is tranquil. It suits the cold stillness of a winter morning.

Pre-dawn monochrome

Backlit desaturation

4) Colour saturation

OK, if we're going to be strictly technical about this, the term 'saturation' refers to how pure a colour is. But over time, and in practical terms, saturation has come to mean how intense or strong a colour appears in an image. Producing saturated images involves more than simply boosting colours in Photoshop – although much can be done that way, with great results, there are many options at the picture-taking stage. Let's consider those first.

The time of day has an impact on colour saturation. Early-morning and late-evening light, with the sun low in the sky and less glare, will produce more intense colours than at other times, as will front lighting rather than side or backlighting.

A polarising filter, by reducing reflections and cutting down on glare, also improves saturation. A polariser has the maximum effect when the camera is at 90° to the sun. Polarisers are simple to use as the effect is clearly visible through the camera's viewfinder – the most obvious one being the increase in saturation of blue skies.

There are a couple of things to watch out for. It's possible to 'over-polarise' a scene, resulting in near-black skies, and also, when using wide-angle lenses (wider than 28mm on a full-frame DSLR or 17mm on an APS-C-sensor), the degree of polarisation can be uneven across the frame.

Of course, you won't always want strong, vibrant, saturated colours. Muted, pastel tones are more subtle, but can be just as effective with the right subject matter, creating an atmosphere of calm and tranquility. Early-morning mist drains colours, and gives a cold, bluish hue to a scene, which you can enhance by tweaking the White Balance in-camera, or later, if you're shooting Raw.

A lot can be done at the processing stage. Experiment with White Balance settings to fine-tune the overall atmosphere and cast. Over the page, we'll show how varying the White Balance of a Raw file can give dramatic results.

Pre-sunrise

Midday

Without polariser

With polariser

Filter choice

■ Types of polariser

There are two types of polariser: circular and linear. This doesn't refer to the physical shape – they're both actually circular – but the way the light is polarised. Make sure you buy a circular polariser for use with your DSLR as linear types interfere with your camera's metering, which can't handle linearly-polarised light.

Colour temperature and White Balance (WB)

Getting to grips with White Balance settings will help you achieve fantastic colours in your shots

DIFFERENT LIGHT SOURCES produce different colour casts, basically in terms of how 'warm' or 'cool' the light is and how much green or magenta is present. For example, a household tungsten light bulb will produce a much warmer light than you will find outside on a cloudy day. While a fluorescent lighting will have a green colour cast.

The warmth or coolness of a light source is referred to as its colour temperature, which is measured in degrees Kelvin (K). The lower the number, the warmer the light – for example, a sunset will have a colour temperature of around 3000K, neutral daylight (noon on a sunny day) is around 5000–5500K, and an overcast sky around 7000–8000K.

Our eyes adapt very quickly and easily to the colour of different light sources and will see a white object as white whether we view it under tungsten light or outside on a cloudy day. To render colour accurately

with a digital camera, however, you will need to set the correct White Balance, which can either be done when taking the picture or when processing the image in your Raw converter. Personally, I'd always recommend shooting in Raw, as it provides a lot more flexibility.

If shooting subjects such as portraits, the correct White Balance is essential for achieving natural-looking skin tones. With landscapes, however, absolute colour accuracy is not always what we strive for – capturing pleasing colours is more what it's all about. So, in the old days of film, landscape photographers would use films like Fuji Velvia for its vibrant colour and use colour correction filters to enhance mood and atmosphere rather than produce neutral, accurate colours. For example, a warm-up filter could be used to enhance the already warm light of a sunset. White Balance settings can be used to achieve similar effects.

Enhance mood with WB

For this series of pictures, I took the same Raw file and applied different White Balance settings to find out which one best suited the overall mood of the picture.

1) DAYLIGHT (5500K) The dusk light was cold and blue. There was just a hint of a glow from the sun below the horizon, picked up by the clouds over the distant headland. The daylight WB has rendered the scene well, with cool blue shadows that suit the mood of the image.

2) CLOUDY (6500K) The cloudy setting has warmed things up and added some magenta. This works well for the sky, but for my taste, has failed to enhance the water and shadows. I suspect a lot of people will like it, though.

3) SHADE (7500K) Too warm and magenta, and doesn't reflect the mood of the scene enough for me.

4) FLUORESCENT (3800K) I actually like this: it's true to the mood of the actual scene, though it is a bit over the top and the sky has lost a lot of 'oomph'.

5) CUSTOM WB (4800K) As a compromise, I went back to the daylight WB and cooled things down a little. I felt that this was a good representation of the mood of the scene, though the sky lacked punch.

1) WB: Daylight

2) WB: Cloudy

3) WB: Shade

4) WB: Fluorescent

5) WB: Custom

Final image

For the final result, I blended the sky from the Cloudy WB into the custom WB image, then faded the sky a little, so that it looked natural with the cooler bottom half. The result was a picture that has cool, blue shadows and a more dramatic sky.

Shooting to create black & white landscapes

The best black & white images come from shooting in colour. Helen Dixon explains her favored technique

I ALWAYS SHOOT my landscapes in colour and then convert to black & white afterwards (turn over the page to read how you can convert your colour images). Doing it this way provides me with the full three channels of information to work with at the Raw processing stage, rather than just one. I do know some people who shoot JPEGs and use the in-camera monochrome setting, often in combination with a red filter to darken greens and blues to give really dark skies, but to get an image with the potential to give the best possible mono results, shoot in colour and convert to black & white on your PC.

You've got to try and visualise a scene in black & white; it's much more challenging than a regular colour landscape. You need a good range of tonal detail, or you will end up with a scene lacking in contrast.

I wouldn't normally shoot an image with a plain blue sky, for example, as you'll just end up with a flat shade of grey. You're looking for an active sky, something with plenty of cloud drama – a scene as a whole that has plenty of shadows and highlights, and separation between foreground and background.

A typical beach scene, for example, doesn't tend to offer much tonal contrast. You've got the sand and the sea, maybe some cliffs, and the sky; each of which is fairly uniform in tone and texture and can end up looking fairly dull in mono. It's for this reason that I tend to gravitate towards country scenes for my

black & white photography, as there's a lot more variation going on in texture and tone.

I also look for more lead-in lines with monochrome; the composition needs to be strong due to the absence of colour. The viewer's eye is more focused on other aspects of the shot, such as shape, form, and texture. Another great thing about shooting landscapes in black & white is that you don't need the best weather. A dark, brooding sky can add a lot of drama to an image, and you don't need to worry about using ND grad filters either, though I do still make sure to use a polarising filter to enhance the sky.

I don't think enough people dedicate time towards black & white photography anymore. You need to see the image in print, hanging on a wall, to really appreciate it. It seems to have that much more power in exhibition than on-screen. The other advantage is that a black & white image will sit nicely on any interior wall, without the risk of it clashing with the colour. Monochrome imagery really does lend itself to display.

BELOW LEFT: East Head, West Wittering. This type of 'scruffy' location works far better in black & white than it would in colour.

BELOW: St Michael's Mount, Cornwall. Lead-in lines are an important visual aid in my monochrome photography, as typified by the cobbled path in the foreground leading towards the distant mount.

RIGHT: Although the tree provides the foreground interest, the clouds really draw the eye in this monochrome image. The stark and barren landscape with bare and lifeless fields all add to the drama. Noise was added to the sky to keep the graininess going throughout the whole scene.

> "Another great thing about shooting black & white is that you don't need the best weather. A dark, brooding sky can add a lot of drama to an image"

How to convert to black & white

There are a number of ways to create monochrome images – we show you the most popular here...

ONE OF THE wonderful things about digital is that it's easy to convert your colour images to monochrome. Photoshop allows for a number of ways to make these conversions, each varying in their level of control and difficulty. This is one reason why we advise shooting in colour and converting the images, rather than set your camera to its monochrome mode. The other reason is that it's impossible to convert a black & white picture to colour, so you're missing out on a photo opportunity. But, most importantly, a colour image holds far more information to help you get the best tonal range for your black & white.

Here, we cover the four most popular methods to convert colour to mono so you can see the difference between each method. We suggest you give each one a try before choosing your favourite.

☑ Adjustable layers

Use *Layer>New Adjustment Layer> Channel Mixer*. It creates a new adjustable layer that can be altered if you change your mind later. Use this technique for Curves and Levels, too

Original colour image

1) Desaturate

This is one of the quickest and easiest routes to convert a colour shot to black & white, and, you've guessed it, the least desirable! Use the shortcut *Ctrl+Shift+U* or *Image>Adjust>Desaturate* to remove colour. Alternatively, slide the *Desaturate* slider to 0 in the Hue/Saturation dialogue box via *Image>Adjustments>Hue/ Saturation*. Looking at the Swatch colour chart, all tones are distinctly muddy – especially the yellows, which appear more mid-grey than light grey. It can be fine for occasional use, but spending a little more time and effort using one of the other methods – as seen on these pages – will yield a much better tonal range in your black & white images.

DESATURATION: The Desaturate method is very quick and easy, but, as you can see here, it produces a flat b&w image with muddy tones.

2) Grayscale

This is a good starting point for most general shots and we have no hesitation in recommending you use this method most of the time. It's a much better way to edit than Desaturate and quickly gives an interesting, high contrast black & white image that often needs little extra work doing to it.

Go to *Image>Mode>Grayscale* to convert the colour photograph to black & white. You can see that the image looks less muddy and that the blues are a little darker. The tonal separation has created an interesting image. From here, you can tweak the image using *Curves* or *Levels*, especially if you select areas like skies or backgrounds beforehand.

GRAYSCALE: Using Grayscale is easy and usually delivers very good results. Here, there is excellent tonal range and good contrast.

3) Black & White Adjustment Layer

This is one of the easiest to use and produces brilliant results. The Black & White adjustment offers users of varied abilities more comprehensive control over an image's tonal range.

Go to *Image>Adjustment Layer> Black & White...* to open the dialogue box and to instantly turn the image monochrome. As well as having a number of presets for controlling contrast to pick from, you have six sliders – each targeting the strength of a specific colour in your image. A good place to start is the *Auto* button, as this alone can deliver attractive results for most images by setting a grayscale mix based on the colour value of the image. You can then use the sliders to tweak the grey values to suit the style of image you want.

It's an excellent tool if you want to darken a blue sky while keeping fluffy white clouds for more impact. Or if you have a scene of yellow flowers amongst green grass – both of which will render a similar shade of grey – and want to target each colour separately. The fine-tuning of your image can be time consuming, but well worth the effort. Be sure to play with all the sliders as you might be surprised at how much the Red slider alters yellows, the Yellow slider alters greens and the Cyan slider affects any blue tones in your scene.

Brightness/Contrast...	
Levels...	⌘L
Curves...	⌘M
Exposure...	
Vibrance...	
Hue/Saturation...	⌘U
Color Balance...	⌘B
Black & White...	⌥⇧⌘B
Photo Filter...	
Channel Mixer...	
Invert	⌘I
Posterize...	
Threshold...	
Gradient Map...	
Selective Color...	
Shadows/Highlights...	
Variations...	
Desaturate	⇧⌘U
Match Color...	
Replace Color...	
Equalize	

4) Channel Mixer Adjustment Layer

Channel Mixer is one of the most powerful ways to convert an image. It's available for Photoshop CS and Paint Shop Pro, with a less sophisticated version in Elements accessible via *Enhance>Convert to Black & White.* The results are very similar to using a red, green or blue filter in front of your lens and you can mix the sliders to create an orange or yellow filter effect. Go to *Image>Adjustment Layer>Channel Mixer* to open the dialogue box. You will have a choice of Red, Green or Blue channels in the Output Channel menu. Now tick the *Monochrome* box to convert to mono. The Red channel is a good starting point, but check out each of them.

You can mix a bit of one channel with another to create new effects. When adjusting the sliders you should aim to keep the combined values of all three sliders to about 100%. For example, Red -20%, Green +140% and Blue -20% – some strange effects can be created by ignoring this! The Constant slider acts as a general brightness control. Try boosting colours beforehand by increasing saturation using *Hue/Saturation*, this will boost contrast significantly in the black & white version. You can even pick a single colour to boost from the *Edit* menu if you like, such as blue.

Levels...	⌘L
Auto Levels	⇧⌘L
Auto Contrast	⌥⇧⌘L
Auto Color	⇧⌘B
Curves...	⌘M
Color Balance...	⌘B
Brightness/Contrast...	
Hue/Saturation...	⌘U
Desaturate	⇧⌘U
Match Color...	
Replace Color...	
Selective Color...	
Channel Mixer...	
Gradient Map...	
Photo Filter...	
Shadow/Highlight...	
Exposure...	
Invert	⌘I
Equalize	
Threshold...	
Posterize...	
Variations...	

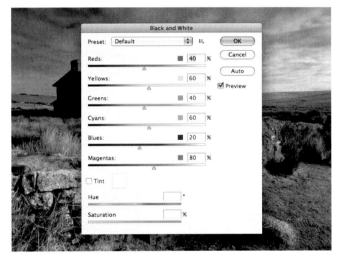

BLACK & WHITE: It's quite amazing to see how by adjusting the different colour channels you can alter the tonality of the image. Go on, have a play!

CHANNEL MIXER: The Channel Mixer is the most involved and time-consuming method but your efforts will be rewarded with the best results.

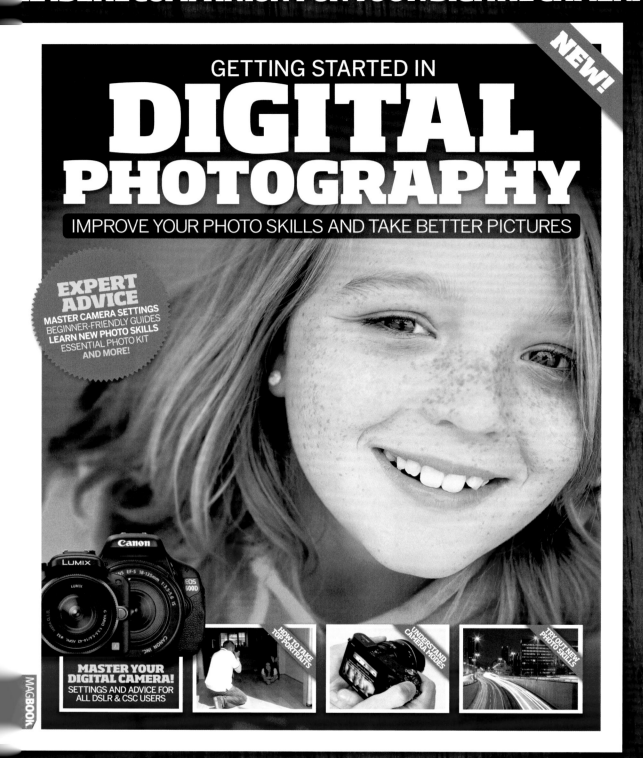

Expert Gems

SEASONAL LANDSCAPES

LANDSCAPES TAKE ON completely different colours and characteristics depending on the season, so make sure to visit your favourite locations at different times of the year.

Winter is the favourite time of year for many landscape photographers. The bare trees mean that the texture of the land itself is fully revealed by the low, raking sun that characterises this time of year. The winter air is clear, and the sun is low enough in the sky to make all-day shooting a possibility. Keep an eye on the weather conditions – a heavy frost or, if you're really lucky, a hoar frost, can create a fairy-tale scene. Take care with metering: the light tones and reflective nature of a frosty landscape can fool the camera's meter into underexposure. Snow looks its best under a blue sky, which can be enhanced with a polarising filter.

Spring is characterised by freshness and an abundance of flowers like daffodils, tulips and bluebells. Spring is also the time for showery weather, which experienced landscape photographers love, as the light immediately after a shower passes is often very dramatic, with the sun bursting through and dark, threatening clouds still in the sky.

Summer is the least favourite season for many landscape photographers. For much of the day, the sun is too high in the sky to provide any textural relief on the scene, the land itself is often obscured by dense foliage and there is a lot of dust and haze in the air. However, all is not lost, and there are shots to be found.

Although there is less variety of flowers than in spring, those that are around have plenty of colour – poppies and sunflowers, for example, or the heather that starts to appear at the end of summer; the time when straw and hay bales start appearing in fields. These make great subjects, especially as they have become one of the great symbols of the British summer.

Autumn is a dream season to shoot. The sun is relatively low in the sky for much of the day, so you can be out taking pictures for hours. The colours are fantastic, so fill the frame with autumnal oranges, reds and yellows. In early autumn, a clear sky and a cold night will often result in early morning mist-filled valleys, rivers and lakes as the sun appears. Mist can look effective if you shoot into the sun but take care to avoid underexposure by setting +1 exposure compensation.

1) Winter wonderland

A layer of frost adds an instant magical atmosphere to your landscape pictures. You'll find a wide-angle lens allows you to fill the frame with the magic of a winter wonderland. The cold weather usually brings a clear blue sky, which complements the crisp, frozen landscape and the pastel colours that can be seen in fields and woodland. Go in low and close with a wide-angle lens and remember to include interest in the foreground.

2) Frozen waterfalls

Partially-frozen waterfalls can make stunning abstract shots. Use a long lens to get close to the base of the fall. Most winter water shots are either flowing water or ice, so include both to add some contrast. A long exposure will soften the water, and create a stark division between the static ice and flowing water.

3) Low-lying sun

This kind of image is worth getting up early for. You can capture a similar image at sunset, but you won't have the appeal of frost. Polarisers perform well on sunny winter days, mainly because the sun remains relatively low in the sky all day long during winter. As well as deepening blue sky it also takes glare off snow. To get the best results, rotate it slowly while looking through the viewfinder. When using a wide-angle lens, take care not to get unevenly polarised skies.

4) Winter sunsets

Although winter light can be harsh, especially in strong sunshine, winter sunsets can be some of the most spectacular of the year. They tend to be very brief, so make sure that you get to your location early, leaving yourself plenty of time to set up and prepare for your shot.

5) A touch of frost

The best time to take winter scenics is shortly after sunrise when the landscape is covered with a coating of frost. If you're willing to wake up early and head into the great outdoors, you could be blessed with a view like this.

Essentials

■ Winter clothing

The best method of staying warm and dry is to wear lightweight layers – thermals, followed by a long-sleeved shirt, a lightweight fleece top, a heavier fleece and finally a decent wind/waterproof jacket. Avoid jeans and instead wear cotton trousers. Hat and gloves are a must and sturdy walking boots to keep your feet warm and dry. In long grass, wear waterproof leggings or gaiters.

Polariser power

An advantage of using a polariser for waterfall shots is that as well as reducing reflections and glare, it has a filter factor of two stops, making it easier to shoot at slower shutter speeds and blur water

1) Spring flowers

Go in low and close with a wide-angle lens to get maximum impact from flowers as foreground interest. Make sure the flowers are in good condition, once petals start to wither and discolour, you've missed your chance. Pin-sharp flowers tend to work best, so try to shoot when they are perfectly still. Experiment with moving flowers and slow shutter speeds too, but make the blur effect really obvious.

2) Chasing rainbows

There is no time like spring for shooting rainbows. When you see dark rain clouds hovering above brightly-lit landscapes, there's a good chance that you'll also see a rainbow. Bracket your shots to give you the best chance of capturing the bands of colour at their best. You could combine these later in Photoshop to create an image with an extended range, which will allow you a greater degree of control over the details, colours and textures of the final image. Finally, a polarising filter will add contrast to the scene, as well as saturating the colours.

3) Bluebell woods

One of Britain's most popular flowers, bluebells usually flower from early April until the end of May. They are predominantly found in the west of Britain, usually in or around woodland, but can also be found near heath, sea cliffs and even mountain tops. When you're deep in the woods, shooting with the sun in front of you can create stunning lighting effects, as it allows you to capture the beams of sunlight penetrating the canopy above, projecting rays of light into the image.

4) April showers

Lots of spring showers offer you the chance to capture scenes packed with moody storm clouds, although you may find yourself waiting for breaks between showers. It can be tricky to get the exposure right if there is a dark sky and bright foreground. A weak ND grad filter can even out the exposure across the frame and add mood. We recommend a 0.3ND or 0.6ND grad.

Essentials

■ **Tripod:** Serious landscape photographers don't set out without a tripod. This will help you with composition, to keep the horizon level and to reduce the risk of unwanted shake, which could ruin your shots. They're also useful if you want to try one of our creative techniques.

■ **Polarising filter:** Polarising filters are ideal for enhancing detail and saturating colours. For the best results, shoot at 90° to the sun. Make sure you buy a circular and not linear polariser.

5) In-camera effects

ZOOM BURST: With your camera on a tripod, set a low ISO rating (eg ISO 100) and a shutter speed of around 1/6sec. Fire the shutter and during the exposure zoom in from the widest setting. Zoom evenly over the exposure time, to reduce the risk of a jagged zoom burst. Experiment with shutter speeds to vary the results.

MOTION BLUR: This technique works really well with bluebells, and the effect is reminiscent of an impressionist watercolour. To achieve this, mount your camera on a tripod with a tilt head. Set an exposure of around one to two seconds and a low ISO rating. Use a remote release (or self-timer) to fire the shutter, and smoothly tilt the tripod head down throughout the exposure.

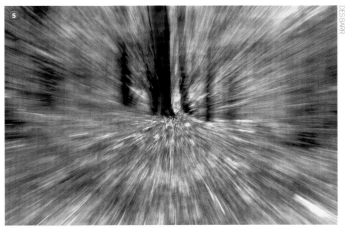

1) Blue skies of summer

We've written it before and you'll certainly read it again, nothing deepens a blue sky better than a polariser. But don't overdo it. On a bright day with good light on the foreground, a slightly underexposed (i.e. dark) blue sky can pack plenty of punch. Pure blue skies tend to disappear by mid-morning.

2) Seaside sunsets

First of all, if you are visiting the east coast, make that sunrise. There are rare coastal areas that loop back on themselves (Hunstanton in Norfolk enjoys sunsets across The Wash) but make sure you head to your location at the right time! Halos around clouds make the very best sunrises and sunsets. Check the exposure via the histogram to ensure you get it right.

3) Evening moods

Evening light stretches very late in summer. The sun hits the horizon at an oblique angle and there is a long afterglow that will produce stunning landscapes long after sunset. Long exposures will capture this soft dreamy time allowing clouds to paint their progress across the sky, emphasising the tranquil mood.

4) Fields of dreams

Take a break from the ubiquitous rape fields and their powerful yellow energy and find out what else is growing in the area you're photographing. Lavender fields are appearing across the country, thanks to the plant's essential oils, said to aid sleep. Keep awake to the possibility of trespassing and don't be tempted to pick the flowers. In late summer, shoot wheat fields in morning or evening light.

5) Bold colours

Let's shake you out of your lavender-induced reverie and smack you between the eyes with strong colours at lunchtime. These poppies look stunning contrasting with the green, and this shot can work even when the sun is high and the thin cloud softens the light like a big studio softbox.

Essentials

■ **UV or skylight filter:**
Although we would always recommend fitting a clear filter to your lens to protect the front element, it's during the summer months that these protective filters will make most difference to your photographs. The ultraviolet filter and the skylight filter both help to remove the haze from summer landscapes. Some film photographers used to fit a gentle warm-up filter to deal with the cool blue cast in shadows on sunny days, but post-processing has made this unnecessary.
See page 60 for more filter advice

1) Misty mornings

Autumn is a great season for shooting misty scenes, and some areas, such as parts of the New Forest, seem to act as 'mist traps', so head out in the early morning to see what the dawn light reveals. Using the long end of a 24-105mm zoom lens, this composition is based around the overlapping shapes of the hills rising out of the mist. A 0.6ND graduated filter helped keep detail in the sky, and a tripod kept everything steady.

2) Nature's mirror

Use reflections in areas of still water such as ponds and lakes to accentuate the season's golden colours. A beautiful display of colour is emphasised by the late afternoon sunshine in this image, taken beside a small brook in the New Forest. An ND graduate filter was positioned over the upper half of the image, to achieve a balanced exposure over the whole picture. After converting the Raw image to a TIFF file, the picture was tone-mapped using Photomatix software to help bring out some detail in the darker areas of the scene.

3) Blanket of colour

Research areas renowned for autumn colour, such as Westonbirt Arboretum in Gloucestershire, with its spectacular display of Japanese maples. Here you'll find colours ranging from bright golds to deep reds. Revisit locations during the season as colours constantly change. Return late season and take advantage of the opportunity to shoot the fallen leaves creating a carpet of colour on the woodland floor.

4) Isolate a single tree

Admit it, you want to climb this tree, don't you? Its gnarly roots and angle of the trunk and branches provide a perfect lead-in to the scene. The composition takes your eye on a journey that your feet want to follow.

5) Blur water

A shutter speed of two seconds or more will blur a woodland stream like this. A long exposure needs a small aperture, giving front-to-back sharpness and the golden leaves add interest to the moss.

Essentials

Wide-angle zoom: A wide-angle zoom lens, such as the Sigma 10-20mm, will allow you to make the most of the majority of autumnal picture-making opportunities. On this page, only the misty mornings shot was taken with a telephoto. When the wider end of your 'standard' zoom isn't wide enough, autumn is a good time to open up even more.

See page 146 for more lens advice

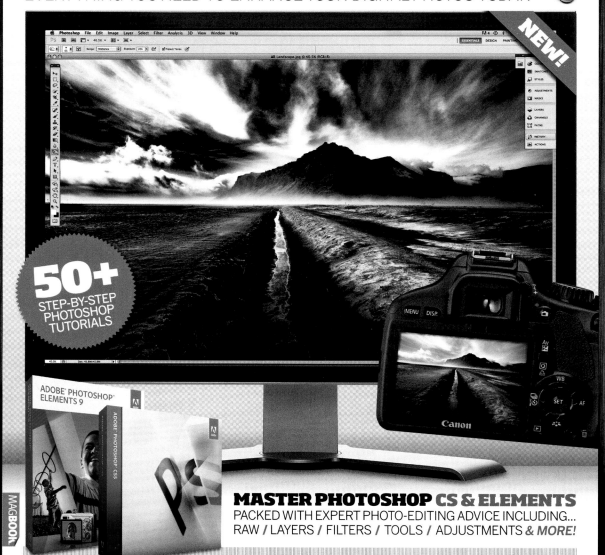

LANDSCAPE PROJECTS

SIMPLE STEPS TO TAKING BETTER PICTURES

IMPROVE YOUR SKILLS
LEARN NEW PHOTO TECHNIQUES!

The world in widescreen

Panoramic images look amazing and, as Mark Bauer explains, they are easier to achieve than ever

THERE'S SOMETHING compelling about panoramic landscapes, especially when you see them as a big print. For me, it's the closest you can get to re-creating the experience of actually being on location to see the vista. As specialist panorama equipment is very expensive, most photographers prefer to create panoramas by taking a series of shots and then stitch them together using Photoshop. However, one should remember that not all scenes lend themselves to a panoramic treatment. Scenes with strong horizontal planes, particularly those that 'flow' naturally from left to right, are ideal. It also helps if there's a strong focal point, such as a building, to break up the horizon line and slow the eye down as it travels across the image. For these shots, I used the distinctive, conically-shaped Colmer's Hill near Bridport as the focal point for my panoramic image.

Set-up

TECHNIQUE WATCH!

■ The rules of panoramas

Panoramas are simple enough to create, providing you follow a few basic rules:

1) Always keep the camera completely level, so the vertical lines don't converge.
2) Set focus, exposure and White Balance manually, so they don't change from one frame to another. To get correct exposure across the whole stitch, take exposure readings from the whole scene you're shooting, average them out and set this in manual mode.
3) Overlap frames by about 25% (see below), as it makes them easier to line up and ensures no areas are missing.
4) Use a remote release and mirror lock-up to ensure all frames are as sharp as possible.
5) Don't waste time between shooting frames, in case something changes – for example, light levels or clouds.
6) Don't use a polarising filter, as the effect will change as you move the camera in relation to the light source.
7) Shoot slightly wider than you think you need, to allow some margin for error with lining up the different frames.

1 Once you have picked out a scene you feel is appropriate for a panorama, it's time to get your camera settings correct (you don't want to be changing them halfway through the series). For this scene, I went for 1/8sec at f/11 (ISO 100).

2 Before you start your 'sweep', choose whether you're going to shoot the pano in landscape or portrait format. If you choose portrait, turn the camera onto its side. Re-check the spirit-level to make sure everything is level.

Kit watch!

■ Tripod & a spirit level

For panoramic landscapes, specialist equipment isn't completely necessary, but there are a few essential items. A tripod is vital for stability and for lining up images, as is a head with a panning action. A remote release will help you keep all frames equally sharp and, finally, a hotshoe-mounted spirit level will keep the camera level (if your camera has an electronic level, you could use this instead). You can buy specialist panorama heads, which pivot around the lens's nodal point (the point where the light paths cross inside the barrel). This prevents lines from converging and makes it easier to line-up frames. It's useful when shooting scenes with lots of straight lines, such as cityscapes, but isn't so vital for shooting landscapes.

Landscapes in portrait!
Try shooting vertically (in portrait orientation) rather than horizontally (in landscape format). It means you take more shots to cover the same area, but there is usually less edge distortion and a better-looking result

Final image
What a view! Now that you've captured the beautiful scene in widescreen, why not consider framing your perfect panorama.

3 To sweep, unlock your tripod's panning function. Take a shot and then start to rotate your camera from one side of the view to the other. Be sure to overlap each frame by around 25% so that there are no missing gaps.

4 Once you've returned home from the location, upload your images to your computer. Next, open Photoshop and then click *File>Automate> Photomerge*, which will then open up a dialogue box with various choices.

5 You have five options for how Photoshop can piece your files together, but for best results stick to *Perspective* or *Cylindrical*. Now click on the *Browse* button and select the images from your desktop or folder. Finally, click *OK*.

6 Your computer will chug away as it processes the files, giving you time for a well-earned cup of tea. After a couple of minutes you will be presented with your panorama. The first thing you'll probably notice is that there's some blank space around the edges of the image.

7 Select the *Crop Tool* from your tool bar and crop the image so you eliminate the blank space from the edges of the frame. Once you're happy with the crop, click the tick icon or hit *OK* and the crop will be complete. Flatten the layers (*Layer>Flatten image*) and save your file.

Exploit the beauty of bluebells

Plan to take a day or two off and head to a bluebell wood to try out one of several creative techniques to capture striking images

THE UK IS the best place in the world to photograph common bluebells – it is estimated that around 70 per cent of their entire population is found here. So, wherever you live in the UK, you will not be far from a bluebell wood. They flower between mid-April and the end of May, but the time when they are at their peak can vary slightly from year to year. Typically, they are at their most photogenic at the start of May, but it is worthwhile making an early visit just to assess what stage they are at – doing so ensures you time your visit correctly and don't miss them at their best.

Weather and timing are key considerations. To be honest, there is no bad weather for photographing bluebells, but a bright overcast day is best. Contrast is low, making it easier to achieve the correct exposure. The quality of light is soft and muted and the colours of woodland flowers and fresh green foliage look naturally more saturated. Early morning and late evening can produce magical light for woodland photography. The light is warmer and the long shadows created add depth to your shots. In bright overhead sunshine, the sun-dappled woodland floor can look attractive to the eye, but the level of contrast can often exceed the capabilities of your sensor's dynamic range. With so much contrast, achieving a good exposure can be difficult, if not impossible – so it is often better to avoid shooting in midday sun. It is also a good idea to visit on a still day, when bluebells will remain still during exposure.

When visiting woodland with large swathes of bluebells; identifying 'the shot' can prove tricky as your choice of composition is almost limitless. To ensure you take great images, a creative eye is vital. Keep composition simple. Avoid clutter, like distracting fallen branches,

and look for interesting woodland detail that you can make a feature of – a mossy stump or large ferns, for instance. Narrow paths winding their way into the distance can be used to draws the viewer's eye into shot.

Lens choice is important so take a range of focal lengths with you. Wide-angles are great for capturing vast carpets of flowers, but often a mid-telephoto – in the region of 50-100mm – is better suited to photographing bluebells. A short telephoto will foreshorten perspective, creating the impression that the carpet of flowers is even denser than it is. This type of focal length is also good if you wish to focus attention on a particularly photogenic group of trees or an individual trunk. A macro lens, or the long end of a telezoom, is ideal to isolate individual flowers.

In overcast light, achieving the right exposure is relatively straightforward. Your camera's multi-zone meter shouldn't have any problems. In early morning or late evening light, it is often preferable to shoot in the direction of the light, so that it 'bleeds' attractively through foliage. However, when shooting towards the light in this way, metering can be deceived and results underexposed. Keep an eye on the histogram and apply exposure compensation if required.

Shutter speeds are often slow in the shade of woodland, so a tripod is essential. For sweeping, wide-angled images of woodland interiors, opt for a small aperture, like f/13. This creates a large depth-of-field which will render everything from front-to-back in focus. However, a shallow depth-of-field will suit some scenes better. For example, isolate a single plant or attractive fern and select a wide aperture like f/4 or f/5.6 to render background flowers as an attractive out-of-focus blue haze.

Other woodland flowers

■ **Wood Anemone:** Widespread and locally common woodland perennial, often growing in large clumps. Its white flowers are beautiful and delicate. Best shot individually in close-up or in context with its woodland surrounding using a wide-angle.

■ **Ramsons:** Often growing among or near bluebells. They smell strongly of garlic and can grow in vast numbers in damp woodland. Very attractive back-lit or in frame-filling close-up. Attach a polarising filter to saturate the colour of the leaves.

■ **Herb Robert:** Common and widespread, its photogenic pink flowers appear from April onwards. Using a macro lens or close-up filter will reveal its delicate beauty. A small silver/white reflector bounces natural light and relieves harsh shadows.

Step-by-step to bluebell magic

Bluebells are unquestionably beautiful, but that is not to say they are easy to photograph. Being such a popular, well-photographed subject makes it even harder to produce original, creative results. Ross Hoddinott provides inspiration by visiting his local woodland in order to shoot a variety of bluebell pictures. His expert advice will help you know what to look for, techniques to try, and the things to avoid, when shooting bluebells.

1 AVOID CLUTTER AND DISTRACTION When I took this image, I was seduced by the vibrancy and colour of the bluebells and overlooked the fallen branches and cluttered woodland floor. Keep compositions clean and simple.

2 LOOK FOR COMPOSITIONAL AIDS Like a winding path or mossy stump that makes for a strong lead-in line. This will give your images a three-dimensional feel. Without this, images may sometimes lack depth and interest.

3 EXPERIMENT WITH DEPTH-OF-FIELD Shallow focus can work well when photographing woodland subjects. Select a wide aperture to diffuse background detail. This will place emphasis on your point of focus.

Standard shot

Standard shot

No polariser

With movement

With zoom burst

With polariser

4 BE CREATIVE Set a shutter speed of one second and move the camera up and down during the exposure to artistically blur the trees. It is a hit and miss technique and may take many attempts to get a result you like.

5 TRY A ZOOM BURST This is another easy, creative technique. Compose your shot using either the zoom's shortest, or longest end. Then, during exposure, smoothly adjust the zoom ring to the opposite end of the lens's range.

6 USE A POLARISING FILTER Doing so will reduce the glare and reflections from foliage and flowers. The filter helps restore natural colour saturation and give woodland images added impact. Note it will increase your shutter speed.

Shoot a misty morning scene

Ross Hoddinott reveals how early morning mist provides a wonderful opportunity to shoot ethereal, magical scenes...

MISTY MORNINGS are one of the key traits of spring. Mist can look magical; filling valleys and hanging atmospherically above fields. By reducing colour and contrast, mist simplifies the look of objects; placing more emphasis on shape and form instead. There are different types of mist and fog, but the most photogenic is 'radiation fog', which forms during clear, still nights when the ground loses heat by radiation, and cools. The ground cools nearby air to saturation point and mist forms. It often stays confined to low ground, forming a thin white layer at the bottom of valleys. When looking at the local weather forecast, look for clear skies and cool, still nights – perfect conditions for mist. Also, look at the forecast for clarity. If clarity is predicted to drop to average or poor during the night, then there is a good chance you will be greeted with mist in the morning. Set your alarm early. Allow enough time to get to your intended viewpoint before sunrise, so that you can get set up and ready in advance of the best conditions. If you are driving, remember your journey will be slower due to the conditions. A high viewpoint, from the top of a

hill or valley, is often best; allowing you to get above the mist to shoot atmospheric views.

Often, objects are reduced to nothing more than a simple silhouette in misty weather. Therefore, look for strong, bold objects to photograph within the landscape – a church steeple, castle ruin, tree or landmark, for example. Longer focal lengths suit misty conditions best, foreshortening perspective and allowing photographers to isolate points of interest. Light scatters and is more diffused in mist, adding to the mystical effect. Often the most dramatic results are from shooting into the light's direction. A medium telephoto lens, in the region of 100mm, will often prove ideal. Mist – like snow – has a habit of fooling a camera's metering system. This is because it is designed to assume that the subject is mid-tone (18% grey). Subjects which are significantly lighter or darker than mid-tone, like a misty landscape, can be exposed incorrectly. TTL metering has a tendency to underexpose mist, rendering it too dark. Consult the camera's histogram screen regularly when shooting mist. If the graph is biased to the left, this is an indicator of

underexposure. Apply positive (+) exposure compensation, to make the image brighter, and then reshoot. You may only need to apply a third, or half a stop of compensation, but in extreme instances, you might have to dial-in a stop or more stops of compensation. Again, use the histogram as your guide.

Having dragged yourself out of bed early to shoot the morning mist, don't overlook the picture potential of smaller, less obvious subjects – for example, dew-laden cobwebs glistening in the morning light.

Weather websites & apps

Outdoor photographers rely heavily on local weather forecasts, especially when waiting for ideal conditions leading to mist. While long-term forecasts aren't always reliable, 24- and 48-hour forecasts are often accurate. Therefore, keep a regular eye on the forecast. Mobile phone apps are an ideal source of information but you should also use websites such as www.metoffice.gov.uk

Time	Weather	Temp	Wind			Visibility
			Dir	Speed	Gust	
2100	☁	4 °C	ENE	8 mph		Very Good
0000	☽	3 °C	ENE	7 mph		Good
0300	FOG	2 °C	ENE	6 mph		Very Poor
0600	FOG	2 °C	ENE	6 mph		Very Poor
0900	☁	4 °C	ENE	4 mph		Good
1200	☀☁	7 °C	NE	7 mph		Very Good
1500	☀☁	7 °C	NE	8 mph		Good

1 I check the local weather forecast daily and noticed that a clear, still night was predicted. Clarity also dropped during the night, so I was optimistic that it would be misty in the morning. I prepared my camera outfit, then set my alarm for just before sunrise.

2 Sure enough, the landscape was shrouded in morning mist. I drove to a high viewpoint, which offered good views over the misty landscape and set up my kit. A telephoto is a good lens choice for mist as it compresses perspective, exaggerating the effect of the mist.

3 Mist simplifies the look of the landscape, giving it a 'layered' effect. I compose my shot, and release the shutter but the result is too dark. By looking at the histogram I can tell the exposure is biased to the left, confirming the image is underexposed.

4 The brightness of mist can fool metering systems designed to assume scenes are mid-tone. Using the camera's exposure compensation button, I dial in one stop of positive (+) compensation to lengthen the exposure time. The result is far better, but the scene lacks a focal point.

5 I scan the landscape for a key point of interest to give my shot more purpose and notice a church tower sticking out above the mist. I recompose the picture to make this my main focal point and also try a vertical composition. The result is a great springtime misty image.

Final image
I tried various compositions but this was my favourite, taken using a short telephoto setting to create an atmospheric landscape image.

Learn how to create a dashing coastal scene

A happy accident led to Lee Frost discovering this stunning abstract technique. Why don't you give it a go?

IT'S FUNNY HOW some photographic techniques come about purely by accident. For example, it's said that solarisation was discovered when American photographer Lee Miller (working as Man Ray's assistant at the time), turned the darkroom light on while a print was still in the developer, causing a partial reversal of the image tones. I can't claim that my latest technique will achieve the same level of fame or popularity, but I discovered it under similar circumstances, while taking pictures on the Northumberland coast just before Christmas. I was planning to shoot a sequence of images for a stitched panorama, so I levelled the camera and scanned the scene I wanted to record. Confident that everything was ready, I tripped the shutter to expose the first frame but, without thinking, I swung the camera to the right, ready to shoot the second frame before the exposure for the first had ended. Annoyed by my impatience, I waited for the image to appear on my camera's preview screen so I could erase it. But when the image did appear, far from being a load of old rubbish, as expected, it looked fantastic – an eye-catching abstract of coloured lines and streaks, more like a painting than a photograph. Surprised by my happy accident, I decided to try and repeat the effect, but this time doing it on purpose. Since then, I've produced a whole series of these images. Not only are they easy and fun, but the results look fantastic. Here's a step-by-step guide so you can try it yourself.

1 First find a suitable location. I live by the sea and favour coastal views because there are defined lines of colour in the scene, created by the beach, then the sea, then the sky. However, any scene containing bands of colour is suitable. In the spring, fields of yellow oilseed rape against blue sky would work brilliantly. The same goes for poppy fields in summer. Urban scenes at night are worth a try too, as the colourful lights will record as streaks. The important thing is that you have clearly defined areas of colour that are wide enough to form strips across your shot. Remember though, that this is an experiment and breaking the rules is allowed!

✅ Steady as you go

Though this technique is all about movement, it's important that your tripod is sturdy and locked off in all directions, other than the pan – otherwise you'll just get a blurry mess

Kit watch!

◼ Tripod head

If you want to produce smooth, consistent results using this technique, you need the right type of tripod head. I've been using a Manfrotto 410 Junior geared head for the past few years. It is great for precise adjustments, but not so great when you want to make bigger, fluid movements of the camera. Fortunately, I recently replaced the geared head with a Manfrotto ball head, which can be unlocked on the horizontal axis, making it easy to pan the camera evenly. Pan & tilt heads are even better because they have arms to adjust the camera on each axis, so you can lock the forward/backward tilt and the vertical adjustment and simply move the camera on the horizontal.

2 If you want the lines and streaks in the image to be straight (or as straight as possible), you need to make sure the camera is level and that it remains level when you pan across during the exposure. I do this by first using the spirit level on my tripod, and then using a second spirit level, mounted on my hotshoe, which helps me to level the camera itself.

3 The streaking is created by moving the camera during exposure, so the shutter speed you use is important. Anything between 0.5secs to two seconds is ideal. To set this, I set the camera to aperture-priority mode and stop the lens down to f/16 or f/22. In low light, such a small aperture may not be necessary, while in bright conditions I often need a Neutral Density filter.

Final image

The final stage, for me, is to crop the image to a square. I feel that the square format adds to the symmetry and makes the composition more balanced and ordered. By always keeping the horizon central, a consistent theme runs through each image, making them work well together.

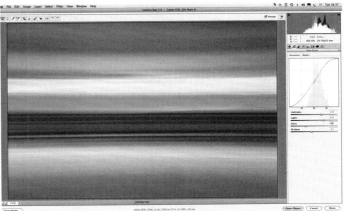

4 Once you're set up and ready, do a few practice runs without taking any pictures. Hold the tripod head or adjustment arm, position the camera to the left of the scene you want to shoot, then smoothly pan from left to right. When you're happy you know what you're doing, try it for real. The results may be a little jerky to begin with, but you'll soon get the hang of it.

5 Back home, download the images to your computer. I shoot in Raw, so the first step is to process them using Adobe Camera Raw. I usually find that adjustments to *Clarity* and *Vibrance* add impact, along with *Tone Curve* to boost contrast. Once opened in Photoshop, I select the sky, make further adjustments to *Levels* and *Curves*, and then do the same to the foreground.

Silhouette a scene

Ross Hoddinott reveals how to add impact to scenes by underexposing major features in the landscape

AS PHOTOGRAPHERS, we are always striving for the 'perfect' exposure, aren't we? However, in practice, is there really such a thing? Exposure can be manipulated for creative or artistic effect – a 'technically correct' exposure won't always produce the most visually pleasing result. Take silhouettes, for example. They are one of my favourite subjects, but technically speaking, a silhouette is the product of poor exposure, with the subject being grossly underexposed. However, there is no denying that they are capable of producing striking, eye-catching results.

A silhouette is when a subject is captured as a black outline, devoid of most or all of its colour or detail. It is the most extreme form of backlighting and, combined with a suitable scene or subject, results can be stunning. Bold, easily identifiable objects, like buildings and trees, work best when photographing silhouetted landscapes – particularly if they are contrasted against a dramatic or colourful sky. They are best captured early morning and late evening, when the position of the sun is low in the sky. By shooting toward the light's direction, objects between you and the light source will be rendered as silhouettes. One of the most appealing things about shooting silhouettes is that they are so easy to achieve and you don't require additional kit. However, as you'll soon see, there are a couple of functions on your camera that can help you to achieve great pictures.

Set-up

1 Bold subjects work best when shooting silhouettes, together with a clean, simple composition. This small church, perched on a tor, proved an ideal subject. I opt for a low viewpoint, allowing me to contrast the building starkly against an uninterrupted sky. I position myself so I'm shooting in the general direction of the setting sun.

2 Using the long end of a 70-300mm telephoto zoom, I crop in tight to the church. As cameras can't predict what effect the photographer is looking for, using multi-zone metering may not provide the best results; in this image it's recorded unwanted detail in the church and foreground. The exposure of 1/2sec at f/11 is too long and the sky is 'washed out' as a result.

Metering technique

Your digital camera's multi-zone metering system is designed to render subjects as a mid-tone. While it proves accurate in the majority of situations, it can struggle when photographing a scene or subject that is considerably lighter or darker in tone. Silhouettes are one subject that can fool metering systems. Although cameras are highly sophisticated, they cannot predict the type of effect you are trying to achieve. Therefore, the camera will normally attempt to render silhouetted subjects as a mid-tone, giving more exposure than is required. This results in skies being overexposed and unwanted detail being recorded in the subject. Thankfully, achieving the correct exposure for silhouettes is simple enough to do by switching to spot metering. It calculates the overall exposure from just a small portion of the frame – usually a central circle covering around 3% of the frame. Aim the spot metering sensor at a bright area of the frame and then press the shutter release button halfway to take a reading. Next, press the Auto-Exposure Lock (AE-L) button to 'lock' your new settings. Recompose your image and release the shutter. The result should be a perfect, inky silhouette. If any detail remains, set a negative value via the exposure compensation dial (start at -1 EV) to reduce the exposure further.

Histograms

When shooting silhouettes, expect corresponding histograms to be more biased to the left of the graph. While normally you would try to avoid histograms showing a high percentage of pixels on the left; in this instance the graph is just reflecting the nature of the technique.

3 When shooting silhouettes, you will normally want to correctly meter for the sky. By basing exposure on a reading from a bright region of the sky, you ensure this will be correctly exposed, while everything else will be underexposed – or silhouetted. The best way to do this is to use the spot metering pattern along with the AE-Lock function.

Final image
Happy with my composition, I decide to experiment with a ten-stop ND filter. With the filter in place, the exposure time was artificially lengthened to 30 seconds. During the exposure, the movement of the cloud was recorded like artistic brush strokes. As the sun finally sets, some colour radiates in the sky, giving my final silhouette even more mood and impact.

4 Aim the spot metering circle at a bright region of the sky and half-depress the shutter release button to take a new reading (mine is 1/30sec at f/11) and lock this setting by pressing the Auto Exposure Lock (AE-L) button. I place my camera on a tripod and, using my new settings, take another picture, which results in this graphic silhouette.

5 While the exposure is correct for capturing a silhouette, the composition could do with some tweaking. Instead of filling the frame with the church, I opt for a wider focal length that allows me to include more sky and interesting cloud. The result is a more balanced picture that shows the church in context with its surroundings.

Shooting star trails

If you're in a remote location, take advantage of clear night skies by capturing stunning star trails

STAR TRAILS are rewarding subjects that can add an element of magic to a landscape shot, revealing the scene in a way that isn't visible to the eye. They allow you to extend the day's potential shooting time, and to get out with your camera – especially if you work through the week and can't get outdoors during the daylight hours in winter. If there's any 'secret' to the technique, it's getting the exposure right, but that's simple when shooting digitally...

✅ Get away from the city
The glow from urban areas is known as light pollution and can be seen from miles away on a clear night. This might not be obvious to the naked eye but will show up clearly on a long exposure

Kit watch!

■ **Manfrotto 055 Pro B Tripod**
You'll need to keep the shutter open for the long exposure and the best way to do that is to use a remote release with a lock to hold the shutter open. This helps avoid inadvertently knocking or moving the camera. A sturdy tripod is important too and a wide-angle lens is handy as it helps you get plenty of sky in the shot. Other than that, star trails don't need any particularly specialist kit. Don't forget plenty of warm clothing though. Even if you're used to being out in cold weather, standing around for half an hour or more in the dark in sub-zero temperatures can bring a whole new level of chilliness, so pack a few extra layers to keep you comfortable.

1 FIND THE LOCATION
If you can, it helps to find your location in advance, in the daylight hours. Midday is a good time to do this for a couple of reasons. One is that it's often dead-time in the landscape photographer's day when the light is too harsh for shooting. The other is that, with the sun to the south, shadows will point north towards where the stars will be circling round Polaris later. Previsualising that will help you create a good composition. You'll need to ensure that you're a decent distance away from major light pollution too.

2 SET UP Pick your night (a night with a half-moon is a good choice if possible) and set up the camera on the tripod. If it's too dark to see properly through the viewfinder, you can take a few shots with a high ISO and wide aperture, gradually making adjustments to fine-tune the composition. Autofocus is unlikely to work in very low light, so you'll need to focus manually – either by using the distance scale or by placing a torch somewhere in the scene to focus on.

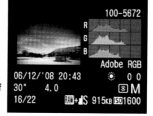

3 METER THE SCENE You can meter the scene before taking the final shot by taking test shots at a high ISO and wide aperture. I'm using ISO 1600 and f/4 here. Set the camera to manual and start with an exposure time of around 20 seconds. Take a shot and check the histogram, then simply alter the exposure time and re-take test shots until the histogram looks correct. After a bit of experimentation I find that one stop underexposed works best.

Final image
I've given the final image more contrast using Curves, adjusted the colour balance to make the tones cooler and applied Unsharp Mask in Photoshop.

4 SETTINGS FOR THE FINAL SHOT When you're happy with the exposure, set the camera to Bulb mode. Select ISO 100 and set a wide aperture. I tend to use f/5.6. Now you can use the exposure time from step 3 to work out the time needed for the final shot, compensating for the change in ISO and aperture by increasing the time. For instance, if you needed a 30 second exposure in step 3: 30secs x 2 (for a one-stop change from f/4 to f/5.6) x 16 (for the change from ISO 1600 to ISO 100) gives a 16-minute exposure.

5 TAKE THE SHOT Turn all lights out, note the time and lock the shutter open with the remote release. Get out some coffee and chocolate, have a break for a while and enjoy staring at the stars. Just don't do what I did and discover at this point that the coffee's back down the road, still in the car! If you need to put a light on at any point to read the time, be careful not to illuminate the foreground at all, as it will show up in the final shot (unless you're deliberately attempting light painting, but that's another topic).

Moonlit landscapes

The brightness of the moon can create other-worldly landscape shots. Here's how to use the moon to your best advantage

JUST BECAUSE THE sun has gone down doesn't mean you can't capture beautiful landscapes. Using moonlight is in fact simpler than photographing at dusk as the light is less variable. Shooting moonlit landscapes is not that different from shooting in daylight, but a lot easier than shooting at sunset, because moonlight is a lot stronger than the last light of the day. That said, you need to pay similar attention to the angle and position of the moon, as you would the sun. A high moon casts strong downward shadows, while a low moon creates long shadows and much softer lighting. It's the optimum light for landscapes and occurs shortly after sunset, just as the moon begins to rise.

Exposure is the main challenge when it comes to moonlight, as it's several thousand times weaker than sunlight. A further complication is the fact that the moon moves fairly quickly, so exposures more than a couple of minutes long can render it a streak in the sky. One solution is to keep the moon out of frame and simply shoot a landscape exposed by its light. Landscapes illuminated exclusively by a full moving moon that softens shadows can make eerie, ethereal pictures. Use too long of an exposure, though, and the light becomes flat. If you want the moon in the picture, but the exposure is too long, take the correct exposure for the foreground, immediately followed by a shorter exposure for the sky, and then merge the two in post-production.

The length of an exposure depends on the intensity of the moon: a full moon on a clear night is great for illuminating landscapes where you want extensive depth-of-field. But if the moon isn't as strong or prominent, you'll find you may need to compromise on depth-of-field by using a wide aperture to reduce exposure times. Remember, though: if you use a wide aperture, focusing is critical.

The best times to shoot are when there's a full moon or during the two days before and after the full moon, when it wanes into and wanes out of its full phase. Note also that layers of cloud affect the exposure, just like it does during the day.

For extra visual interest, try shooting with a river, lake or sea in the foreground, so you can capture the light beams glistening off the surface – you'll find that the reflected light also brightens the whole scene. You could also introduce flash or a torch into your shoot, using it to paint the foreground.

When setting up your camera, apply the same techniques already explained in this guide: use Bulb or manual mode, work out the exposure, focus manually if possible and fire the shutter using a remote release. When working out the exposure for a moonlit scene, multi-zone metering works well. Then follow the technique explained previously: take a test shot in aperture-priority mode at your highest ISO rating and widest aperture to give yourself a base shutter speed, then use reciprocity failure to work out the exposure for a decent aperture and low ISO rating. Alternatively, switch to spot metering and meter off the brightest part in the scene, then add two stops of extra exposure, because the metering system will otherwise render your highlights as a mid-tone.

Once you've mastered star trails and moonlit landscapes, why not apply the principles to shooting auroras, meteor showers or even invest in the equipment needed for deep-space photography?

RIGHT: MOONLIGHTING: For every exposure of this scene, the f/stop and ISO had to be adjusted to keep the shutter speed between 15 and 30 seconds in order to freeze the moon's motion. BELOW: This shot of Swaledale comprises a four-minute exposure for the foreground and a 30-second exposure for the sky.

JOHN PATRICK

Reciprocity law

With low-light photography, it's important to remind yourself about the interchangeable relationship between shutter speeds and apertures so that you can work out the required exposure. It takes a bit of brain power, but there are Smartphone apps that can help calculate equivalent exposures. Basically every time you stop down your aperture, you need to double your shutter speed, so if you go from f/4 to f/5.6 the shutter speed needs to double from, say, two seconds to four seconds. While reciprocity law failure (when the camera fails to accurately meter a scene in low light) is less common with digital than film, you may find you need to add an extra stop or two of exposure to ward off underexposure.

GARY McFARLAND

How to shoot the moon

For those of us who don't have the resources for deep-space photography of the Milky Way galaxy, the nearest thing we have to the mysticism of space is the moon. You don't need any special equipment to photograph the moon, only what you'd normally use for most night photography but a decent telephoto zoom would be an asset, in particular those extending to at least 300mm. If you don't have a suitable lens, you could invest in a teleconverter to extend the reach. Remember that an APS-C camera has a crop factor of x1.5, so the equivalent focal length of a 200mm lens is 300mm.

It's easy to underestimate the moon's brightness, which is why getting the exposure correct can be quite tricky. Most first attempts at lunar photographs result in an overexposed circle where the moon should be. The first step to avoiding this is to pick a spot where there is no ambient light from traffic or streetlights, on a clear night, with no cloud. There is a little trial and error needed to get the perfect exposure as it changes depending on the shooting conditions, but set your camera to manual mode and use 1/250sec at f/8 (ISO 100) as a starting point. Take a series of bracketed exposures (in one-stop increments) around this setting and review them on the LCD monitor. We'd recommend you change the shutter speed rather than the aperture. Depending on the phase of the moon, its brightness, your location and the atmospheric conditions, you may find you need to lengthen or shorten the exposure to capture enough tonal detail on the lunar surface. Position your focus point over the moon, lock on to it using autofocus and then switch to manual focus to stop it hunting.

LEE FROST

Use a remote release or the self-timer to minimise the risk of shake blurring the result.

You're likely to have to crop the image in Photoshop and do a little work on the tonality by adjusting the Levels to draw out more detail on the moon's surface.

Try 5 issues for £5

Master your DSLR with this trial offer!

Claim 5 issues of *Digital SLR Photography* magazine today for £5!

You'll get the next 5 issues delivered direct to your door and if you like what you see, your subscription will continue at the LOW RATE of £21.49 every 6 issues. That's a **saving of 10% on the shop price** – only £3.58 an issue, instead of £3.99 in the shops!

If *Digital SLR Photography* isn't for you, simply write to cancel, and pay no more than £5!

YOUR GREAT DEAL

☑ **5 issues for £5** to start your subscription

☑ **FREE delivery** of every issue

☑ **SAVE 10%** on the shop price if you choose to continue reading

☑ Improve your DSLR skills with our expert advice

Get your 5 issues for £5 today

☎ **PHONE: 0844 249 0482** Please quote offer code below

🖥 **ORDER ONLINE: www.dennismags.co.uk/dslr**

PHOTOSHOP TECHNIQUES

CREATIVE PHOTOSHOP TECHNIQUES FOR YOUR LANDSCAPES

Breathe life into flat photos

Want to create an HDR effect but don't have Raw files or a set of bracketed exposures? Shadows & Highlights could be just the tonic!

WE ALL HAVE images that didn't quite render the scene how you remember it. Maybe the sky's not as moody, or the ground is too dark, or maybe the overall appearance of the image lacks contrast or is badly exposed. Well, Shadows & Highlights can resurrect these images. This nifty adjustment is a fantastic photographic tool, which is often overlooked by users since dedicated HDR software like Photomatix and Photoshop actions became available from third-party companies. In the simplest terms, the adjustments allows you to recover detail from over- or underexposed areas by adjusting the Highlights or Shadows controls respectively, or you can improve the overall tonal range using the Midtone Contrast slider. It's really very simple. The key to success with Shadows & Highlights is subtlety. As with any process that plays with tonal range, HDR included, shadows and highlights can produce photographic Frankensteins if used too eagerly. So, why not give it a go – the controls may seem daunting at first, but after a little experimentation and with a better understanding of what can be achieved, you may find you'll be using this feature regularly.

Hot keys

Alt to reset
When working in the Shadows & Highlights, hold down **Alt** to change the **Cancel** button to a **Reset** button in case you want to take the filter back to its default settings. You can also uncheck **Preview** to toggle between the blurred and original image.

1 DUPLICATE ORIGINAL Our chosen image is a bit lifeless, yet clearly has potential texture in the sky and detail in the foreground that could be pulled out using Shadows & Highlights. First, create a duplicate layer from the original by going to *Layer>Duplicate Layer...*, naming the layer accordingly for reference later.

2 SHADOWS & HIGHLIGHTS On the duplicate layer go to *Image>Adjustments> Shadows & Highlights...* As the image is generally flat, concentrate on the *Shadows* and *Midtone* Contrast, with only minor adjustments to the *Highlight* field. At this stage you want to be focusing more on getting the foreground right.

3 DUPLICATE ADJUSTED LAYER Now duplicate this edited layer with *Layer> Duplicate Layer...* Then add a Layer Mask by going to *Layer>Layer Mask>Reveal All* or by clicking on the *Add Layer Mask* icon at the bottom of the Layers palette. The purpose of the Layer Mask is so the next edit only affects the sky area of this layer.

4 ADD A GRADIENT Click on the Layer Mask thumbnail and select the *Gradient Tool*, ensuring the foreground and background colours are set to the default black and white. With the *Shift* key held down to ensure a straight line, click near the horizon and drag, letting go at the top of the image. This adds a gradient to the mask.

5 CREATE A STORMY SKY With the mask in place, any work done will only affect the sky area. Open *Shadows & Highlights* as instructed in step 3, but this time we want to work mainly on the *Highlights* and *Midtones Contrast* to pull all the detail back into the sky. You may want to increase the *Black Clip* to improve contrast.

6 REDUCE SATURATION One final tweak is to remove some of the colour to enhance the storm-like appearance of the image. With the top layer active, go to *Layer>New Adjustment Layer> Hue/Saturation...* and reduce the *Saturation* slider by around 20%, then click *OK*. Now save as a Photoshop file (.PSD), to preserve all the layers.

A storm is brewing!
From flat to fantastic:
Shadows & Highlights has
pulled out lots of detail that
lay hidden in the JPEG.

Add a digital graduated filter

Using Photoshop for an ND grad effect is easy when you know how...

PHOTOSHOP CAN BE used to replicate most effects achievable in-camera, including the results you get from using graduated filters. Photoshop is not an alternative to optical filters, however; it's a complementary skill. Use it to produce images that were not possible to achieve on location or when you forget your grad. In this step-by-step tutorial, we show you how to create your own stunning graduate filter effect using Adjustment Layers and we introduce you to Gradient Fill, Gradient Editor, Color Picker, Blending Modes and Photo Filter. Photoshop Elements 4.0 was used here, but more recent versions and Photoshop CS versions are suitable, too, though you may find features located differently.

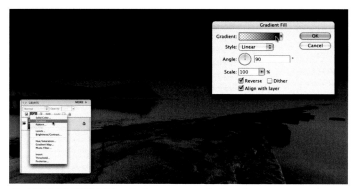

1 ADD A GRADIENT The aim is to create a similar effect to a conventional grad filter, but using a series of digital graduated layers instead. Create your first gradient by clicking the *Create Adjustment Layer* icon (⊘), situated at the top of the Layers palette, and scrolling to *Gradient*, which opens the *Gradient Fill* window.

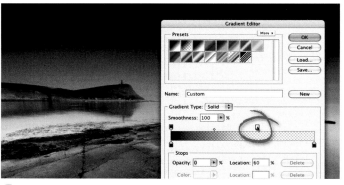

2 REFINE THE GRADIENT In the *Gradient Fill* window, tick Reverse so the gradient runs top to bottom, then click anywhere within the *Gradient* field (situated top) to open the *Gradient Editor* sub-window. The sliders at the top of the visible gradient control opacity, and moving the *White* slider will increase the transparent ratio of the gradient.

3 CHANGE THE COLOUR The sliders at the bottom of the gradient control colour, the left representing black. Click on the black slider and note that the colour now appears in the field below, clicking here opens the *Color Picker* sub-window. Use the vertical spectrum (centre) and the main window (left) to select the desired colour then click *OK*.

4 BLEND THE LAYERS Click *OK* in the subsequent windows to apply the gradient, then choose *Multiply* from the *Blending Mode* menu situated to the top of the Layer palette (inset) to create a more natural merging of the gradient to the original image. This *Adjustment Layer Gradient* can be tweaked at any time by selecting it in the Layers palette.

5 REPEAT THE PROCESS It's quite often necessary to create more than one gradient layer to build up the filter effect. Repeat steps 1 and 2, this time creating a gradient that is black to transparent. Then, choose *Soft Light* in the *Blending Mode* menu and reduce the layer's *Opacity* (inset) creating a natural darkening effect that can easily be adjusted.

6 ADDRESS THE FOREGROUND For this image, the final gradient layer is going to add a subtle fall-off on the rocks leading out of the image to the bottom of the frame. Again, repeat steps 1 and 2, this time leaving the Reverse box unticked so the gradient runs from bottom to top. Once again, set the *Blending Mode* to *Soft Light* and reduce the *Opacity*.

Final image
After a few minutes in Photoshop, we've managed to give a plain sky extra interest.

Adding the final touch with *Filter>Adjustments>Photo Filter*

7 USE PHOTO FILTERS Photoshop Elements and CS have mood filters that can change the overall tone of your image, much like using a coloured gel or filter on your digital camera. This handy action, found in the top menu under *Filter>Adjustments>Photo Filter*, has several presets including Warming, Cooling and Sepia or you can choose to manually select a tone via the *Color Picker*. The intensity of the selected tone can be adjusted by the *Density* slider to allow for some very subtle effects, giving far greater control than that of an optical lens filters. When you've finished adding a grad effect to an image, it's well worth the time trying some of these out to see if the image can be improved upon further.

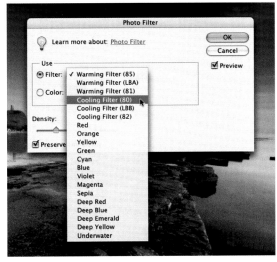

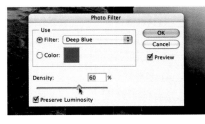

ABOVE: Choose from a range of preset filters available in the Photo Filter function or use the Color Picker to customise.

RIGHT: FINAL COLOUR SELECTION Although happy with the results of the grad filter effect, we found the image could be improved even more using the Photo Filter action. After experimenting, we decided upon the Deep Blue preset filter set at about 60% Density as it made the overall mood of the image slightly cooler – we think it works better here.

Create a misty morning

The Gradient Tool is ideal for adding an eerie wintry feel to your images. A few other little tricks are necessary to pull it off, though

MIST IS ONE of those elusive elements that rarely appears when you want it to but when it does it can transform the atmosphere of your landscapes. Now this step-by-step is no substitute for the real thing, but it can be used to improve your current landscape images or to occasionally relieve you having to wake early on a winter morning to search for natural mist.

Deep valleys and rolling hills make beautiful scenes for misty landscapes, as do frost-bitten fields. Refer to some example images before you try this technique just to see how mist naturally acts in different situations. Mist tends to look gradually heavier the further it is away from you, which is why you'll notice we handle the image treatment in sections: background, middle-distance and foreground, with each one having a different intensity of mist.

Hot keys

■ **Set foreground & background color**

When using Layer Masks or the Gradient Tool, use the X key to change between the foreground and background colour, which is set to black & white as default.

X

Original

1 ADD A GRADIENT Use *Layer>New>Layer...* to create a layer above the original. Select the *Gradient Tool* and ensure it's set to *Linear* gradient in the options bar, and that the foreground colour is set to *White* and the background to *Black*. Click and hold, then drag from the top of the image to just under the horizon to create the background layer of mist.

2 REVEAL THE TREE In reality, the mist would be behind the tree. To give it this appearance, add a *Layer Mask* by clicking the icon in the Layers palette (circled). Next, select the *Brush Tool*, set to *Black* and an appropriate size, and begin to work over the tree, removing the mist. If you go too far, you can change the brush colour to White and paint over the area to bring back detail.

3 FOCUS ON THE MIDDLE-DISTANCE To add fog to the middle-distance, create another new layer via *Layer>New>Layer...* Use the *Gradient Tool* with the same settings, and draw a line from the top to the bottom of the image and release to create an even gradient across the frame. Reduce the *Opacity* by changing the amount to *50%* in the Layers palette (circled).

4 ADD FOREGROUND MIST To create eerie foreground mist, again add a new layer (*Layer>New>Layer...*), then go to *Filter> Render>Clouds* to fill the layer with a textured cloud effect. Use *Image>Adjustments>Levels...* and the black and white sliders to boost the contrast on the image. Finally, change the layer *Blend Mode* to *Screen* to make the layers interact.

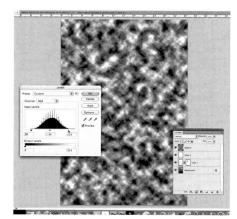

5 ADJUST PERSPECTIVE To add perspective, go to *Edit>Free Transform>Scale* and reduce down to the foreground area by dragging the top-centre tab. Before applying, change the transform to *Perspective* and drag one of the bottom corner tabs outside the pasteboard until you're happy. You may need to zoom out to move the tabs out far enough, as shown here.

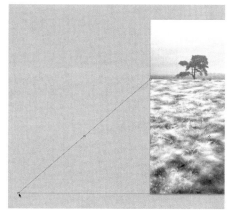

6 TWEAK COLOUR & CONTRAST Create two adjustment layers by selecting the icon at the bottom of the Layers palette (circled). First, create a *Hue/Saturation* adjustment layer, and use the *Saturation* slider to desaturate the colours slightly, and, finally, create a *Brightness/Contrast* adjustment layer to boost the contrast sufficiently to enhance the appearance of diffused misty light.

A mist opportunity!

A few simple steps are
all it takes to add a
touch of mist to your
landscape images.

Bland to beautiful: learn how to replace a sky

Improve your landscape images ten-fold with this simple technique where you can swap an uninspiring sky for one with more drama

THE BRITISH WEATHER is well known for not doing quite what you want it to and rarely do all of the elements play ball when it comes to landscape photography. You can be perched above a beautiful vista, camera ready on a tripod and remote in hand, but the one thing you can't do much about is a bland sky. All is not lost, though: in a few simple steps you can easily replace the sky and transform your landscapes from drab to dramatic. You'll need to find a replacement sky to swap in, of course, and it's worth keeping a small library of skies in a folder on your computer for such occasions. Try to shoot a range of different skies from different times of the day with different cloud formations: it makes it a lot easier when the sky you are replacing is of a similar colour and time of the day to the replacement. Often trial and error is the key to finding the right sky for your scene, so it's best to have as much variety as possible.

1 SELECT THE SKY Open your image, choose the *Quick Selection* Tool and begin painting across the sky. If your image contains objects on the horizon, as ours does, you will need to zoom in and adjust your brush size in the options toolbar to make a more accurate selection. If you select an area by mistake, simply hold down the *Alt* key and erase the selection. Once happy with your selection, go to *Select>Inverse*.

2 REFINE THE SELECTION Go to *Select>Refine Edge* to bring up the options window. Click *Default* and the sky will appear white. Using the *Contract/Expand* slider, adjust the selection so that it closely follows the lines of the horizon. You can alter the preview by selecting one of the preview options at the bottom. Once done, click *OK*. Then go to *Select>Inverse* again and press the *Backspace* key to remove the sky.

3 BRING IN THE NEW SKY Open your replacement sky image in a new window and, using the *Rectangular Marquee Tool*, select the sky only. Copy your selection by going to *Edit>Copy* and close your sky image without saving. Head back to your original image and paste the sky in by going to *Edit>Paste*. It's very unlikely that your new sky will fit your image straight away, so don't worry if this is the case.

4 ADJUST THE PROPORTIONS Go to *Edit> Transform>Scale* and, holding down the *Shift* key, drag the corners of the sky image out to match the width of your landscape. Once happy, click on the Tick at the top, or press the *Enter* key. Use the *Move* Tool to line the sky up so that it completely covers the white area of the image. Don't worry about any overlap onto the horizon at this point.

5 CREATE A GRADIENT Click on the *Add Vector Mask* button in the Layers palette. Select the *Gradient Tool* and make sure that the black to white gradient is selected. On the image, click and drag the line from just below the horizon to the top of the sky, then release the button. This part involves trial and error, but you can repeat as many times as you need to until you are happy with the effect.

✓ **New horizons**
The sky typically gets brighter the closer to the horizon it is. Bear this in mind when applying your gradient. If the gradient is too low or too hard, then the effect will lack realism, which is important

Final image
We think you'll agree that the new sky adds some much needed drama to the original image.

ISTOCK PHOTO

6 TIDY UP THE HORIZON Some of your new sky will still overlap onto the landscape, so to tidy this up, select the *Brush Tool*, lower the *Opacity* to 25% and set the brush's *Hardness* to 25% in the options toolbar. Select *Black* as your foreground colour and brush over the horizon, building up areas that you wish to reveal. If you make a mistake, simply select White as your foreground colour and brush back over.

7 ADJUST THE CONTRAST In the Layers palette, click on the *Create new adjustment layer* button and select *Levels* from the menu. First make sure that the adjustment is clipped to the layer below only by clicking the button at the bottom of the Adjustments palette. Then adjust the contrast of your sky to match the rest of the image using the middle (mid-tones) level slider. Once done, go *File>Save As*.

Workflow tip

Quick Selection

The Quick Selection Tool was released with the launch of Photoshop CS3 and Elements 6, and has featured in all versions since. It works by detecting contrast differences, and makes a selection based on this: ideal for separating skies from horizons. Just be aware of horizons with low cloud or mist cover, as the tool may struggle to separate them accurately.

Make the year a blur with a four seasons special

Give your seasonal landscapes a creative twist with this simple but striking motion blur technique

EVERY SEASON offers new possibilities to photograph striking colour-filled landscapes, whether it be ruby-red poppies, sun-kissed oilseed rape, blankets of burnt orange leaves or black & white scenes in winter – you're never short of opportunities. While there are a million and one ways to photograph these classic scenes, each as beautiful as the other, we wanted to try a technique that would give seasonal scenes a fresh, artistic appeal. If you've read our *Landscape Projects* section, you would have come across motionscapes where you pan the camera across a coastal horizon to create streaks of colour. This technique is very similar but applies vertical streaks instead, using Photoshop. You can do a similar technique in-camera using a three-way pan-tilt tripod head to pan the camera up and

down in a fluid movement, but it will blur the entire image, whereas here we only want to blur half of it. Plus, while the purists may be cursing, the effect is much easier to control, with better results, using Photoshop's Motion Blur filter.

After some trial and error it was clear that to get the best results for our seasonal quadtych (series of four images), we'd need images where there was as much interest in the top of the frame as the bottom, otherwise you wouldn't be able to tell what was blurred or in focus. We found that the best scenes seemed to be forests or landscapes where trees fill the height of the frame, so with this in mind we rummaged through our hard drives for suitable images for spring, summer, autumn and winter.

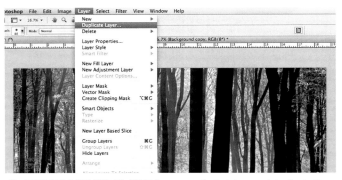

1 CREATE A DUPLICATE LAYER Open your first picture and duplicate the image by clicking on the *Background Layer* in the Layers palette and going to *Layer>Duplicate Layer*, or by dragging it down to the *Create a new layer* icon at the bottom of the Layers palette. From now on you'll only be working on this duplicate layer. Leave the original image untouched.

2 APPLY MOTION BLUR Click on *Filter>Blur>Motion Blur* to open the filter's dialog box. As you want to apply a vertical blur, set the *Angle* to 90° by either typing the amount in or moving the angle finder. You'll notice that by clicking and dragging on the angle finder the direction of the blur will change in the preview screen.

3 INCREASE THE STRENGTH Adjust the *Distance* slider to increase the strength of the blur effect. The bottom of the image needs to be heavily blurred but not to the point that the subjects become unrecognisable. It will be different for every image (we used 409 pixels). When you're happy, click *OK*.

4 APPLY A LAYER MASK To add a Layer Mask to the blurred image, click on the *Add Layer Mask* icon at the bottom of the Layers palette. You'll notice this adds a white box next to your image in the Layers palette. Then select the *Gradient Tool* from the toolbar or press *G*.

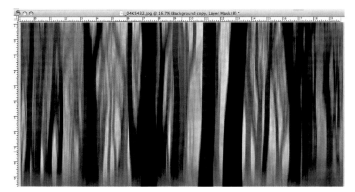

5 MASK OFF THE BLUR With the *Gradient Tool* and the Layer Mask selected (black lines appear around the mask's corners when it's activated), click at the top of the image and drag the cursor down to the point where you want the blur to start.

Final image
Print the pictures out and frame them for the wall or why not try having them made into canvas prints or acrylics for a different look.

6 REPEAT What you've done is create a gradient in your Layer Mask that allows the blur to graduate through your image. You can change the graduation by repeating step 5. You'll find the images look better if the blur is heavier at the bottom of the picture than the top.

7 APPLY THE TECHNIQUE TO ALL SEASONS Repeat steps 1 - 6 with the other three images of your choice. We've picked a colourful autumn woodland scene, bright sunshine passing through trees for summer and a black & white picture of a snowy forest.

Create the ten-stop effect

Neutral Density filters are brilliant but require dedication to get consistently great results. Here's a quick technique for those who want to trial the effect or don't have time to attempt the real thing

FOR ANY OF YOU who haven't been lucky enough to use one yet, the ten-stop ND filter is amazing! By significantly lengthening a camera's exposure, the filter allows the camera to capture motion so clouds are rendered as streaks and water becomes a fine mist – it's truly magnificent, but it takes skill and patience to perfect. As great as this technique is, often success depends on the location, and with exposure times usually running to more than an hour it demands extreme dedication and time – two things we can't always spare in our hectic schedules.

There is, however, a shortcut to getting a very similar effect using Photoshop's Blur filters, and while it may not be one for the photo-purist, it can produce a very convincing comparison when combined with the right kind of image. Feel free to experiment on any image but it's usually coastal scenes that produce the most dramatic results. For further inspiration of what images might work, it's worth looking at contributor Lee Frost's motion studies project (www.leefrost.co.uk) taken with an actual ten-stop ND filter.

How to use...

Layer masks

A Layer Mask allows you to hide detail from the layer it's applied to, revealing the image beneath, without erasing it. When the Layer Mask is selected, simply add the colour black to the mask to hide image detail and change to the colour white to restore the detail. Use the **X** key to quickly switch between the colours.

Original

1 CREATE DUPLICATE LAYERS First create a duplicate layer from the Background image by going to *Layer>Duplicate Layer...*, naming the layer accordingly – here the layer is called 'Water Blur'. Then click on the *Add Layer Mask* icon at the bottom of the Layers palette to add a Layer Mask. Repeat this process to create an additional duplicate layer – we name this one 'Sky Blur'.

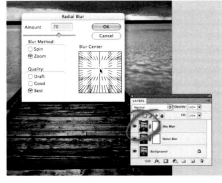

2 APPLY RADIAL BLUR On the sky layer, ensure the image thumbnail is selected (circled), then go to *Filter>Blur>Radial Blur...* In the Radial Blur window, make sure that the *Blur Method* is *Zoom* and *Quality* is set to *Best*. Next, enter a large Amount – no less than 50 – and move the *Blur Center* to an area where the horizon would roughly be positioned on the image, and click *OK*.

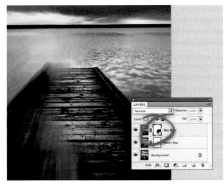

3 HIDE FOREGROUND BLUR The radial blur should only affect the sky portion of this layer, so click on the Layer Mask thumbnail in the Layers palette (circled) and, with the *Brush Tool* set to a large soft-edged brush, paint across the foreground area with *Black* to hide the blur in areas you don't want it applied to yet. Switch to a smaller brush when working near the horizon.

4 BLUR THE WATER Switch to the water layer by clicking on it. Add a Radial zoom blur, with all the settings as in the previous step, but reducing the *Amount* down by half to 35, just to make the cloud reflections more realistic. Then go to *Filter>Blur>Gaussian Blur...* setting the amount to no more than 15 pixels. This adds a hazy sheen to water common with many long exposure images.

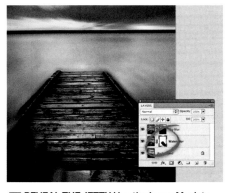

5 REVEAL THE JETTY Use the Layer Mask to reveal static areas, in this case the jetty. Click on Layer Mask (circled), then select the *Polygonal Lasso Tool* and draw a selection around the edge of the static area. Once complete go to *Select> Modify> Feather...* and apply 1 pixel to avoid a harsh edge to the selection. Take the *Brush Tool*, still set to black, and paint over the selection.

6 CONVERT TO MONO To convert the image, go to *Image>Adjustments>Black & White...* and click *OK* to use the default settings. Conversions from colour to mono often leave an image looking a little flat, so use *Image>Adjustments>Levels...* to add contrast. Use the Black point and White point sliders (circled) to boost the blacks and whites respectively, taking care not to burn out any detail.

Poetry in motion!
With just a few steps you could add this beautiful atmospheric effect to your landscape images.

Get dramatic with your black & white conversions

Get to grips with the skills that you need to create a stunning black & white picture, with a technique that goes beyond the basics and is guaranteed to add impact to images

WHEN SHOOTING LANDSCAPES, most of us give little thought to how results may appear in mono. This is understandable as, for most of us, the vast majority of shots we take will remain in colour. Now we're not suggesting that in future you imagine how every scene you shoot might look in black & white, but we would suggest you consider it from time to time. Shooting images to convert to mono is somewhat of a discipline and when you do plan to capture a scene with the intention of making it monochrome, you should bear in mind factors that may affect the impact of your picture, or the lack thereof, once it's converted. To stop an image appearing lifeless once the colour is stripped away. You need to pay particular attention on the composition, tonal range, shapes and foreground interest.

First of all, it's worth avoiding areas with highly saturated colour, like sunsets, or fields of bluebells, poppies and canola, because a black & white image simply won't do them justice. Remember that every colour has its own shade of grey when converted to mono, so you're looking for scenes that show a range of lights and darks, otherwise you risk the image looking flat and lacking tonal range.

Form is a vital ingredient of mono landscapes, so look for scenes with textures, strong lines and bold shapes that can help create contrast in black & white, and foreground interest that can lead the eye in to the scene. Wet rocks are brilliant for achieving contrast as you can get specular highlights from where the sun bounces off their wet surface. Rough weather often adds drama to scenes: stormy skies are wonderful. You should avoid cloudless skies, as these give grey, lifeless results. If clouds are more wispy than substantial, you can use Photoshop to selectively adjust the exposure; darkening them to add some drama.

While directional light is better for creating contrast, Mother Nature doesn't always bless us with the perfect photography conditions, but don't worry, as we'll show you how you can selectively adjust the exposure using the Dodge and Burn Tools to transform your mellow mid-tones in to highlights and shadows for extra impact.

Converting your image to mono in Adobe Camera Raw or using a black & white adjustment layer are both brilliant ways to get great results (both of which we'll cover in detail later), but we shouldn't neglect the Channel Mixer, which was a favourite method for many until CS3. It's a step up in quality and a lot more controllable than a simple grayscale conversion. And while not as advanced as the other methods, it allows you to work with the colour information in the image to enhance the tonal range more precisely, and is still one of the best ways to get extreme contrast.

1 PROCESS THE RAW FILE Open your image using Photoshop Adobe Camera Raw. The first thing that you need to do is to make any necessary exposure adjustments to get the image how you want it to look. For this image, we adjust the *Exposure* slider by adding a positive value to lighten the picture and the *Blacks* slider to slightly increase contrast.

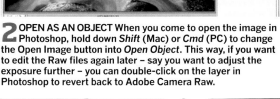

2 OPEN AS AN OBJECT When you come to open the image in Photoshop, hold down *Shift* (Mac) or *Cmd* (PC) to change the Open Image button into *Open Object*. This way, if you want to edit the Raw files again later – say you want to adjust the exposure further – you can double-click on the layer in Photoshop to revert back to Adobe Camera Raw.

3 APPLY AN ADJUSTMENT LAYER Duplicate the layer (*Layer>Duplicate Layer*) and rasterize the image so that you can edit it by clicking on the image. Click *OK* in the dialogue box. Next, go to *Layer>New Adjustment Layer>Channel Mixer* to convert your image to black & white. Using an Adjustment Layer means that if you want to undo your conversion, you can just delete the layer as you haven't affected the original image.

4 CONVERT TO BLACK & WHITE To start with, click on the *Monochrome* box to turn the image black & white. Next, use the sliders to adjust the *Red, Green and Blue* channels to improve the contrast. For the best results, avoid 'clipping' any highlights or shadows by making the total value of the sliders 100%. You can check this under the sliders, where you'll see the total amount changing as you modify the colours.

5 AVOID 'CLIPPING' AREAS This is how not to do it. See how the total value is 200% – while the shadows are well exposed, the highlights have been clipped and we've lost detail in the sky and the water. It's all about finding the right balance. If you find you have a couple of hotspots or dark areas that you can't get right using channels, you'll be able to correct these in the next step – just try to avoid doing it in excess.

Final image
By using the Dodge and Burn Tools you can bring over and underexposed areas back from the brink for a brilliant mono result.

6 MAKE LOCAL ADJUSTMENTS Click back to the Layers palette and on to the duplicate layer. If you have some areas that need lightening a little, select the *Dodge Tool* from the toolbar. You will then need to select a large, soft brush (we use a diameter of 900px and 0% *Hardness*) from the Options bar (the top toolbar) land select *Shadows* from the *Range* drop-down menu, set the *Exposure* as low as 4% and check *Protect Tones*.

7 LIGHTEN DARK AREAS Brush over the area you want to lighten in soft, fluid movements. If your brush is too hard or your exposure is too high, you'll find you'll make circles over the areas you're brushing on. Try to build the effect up softly. Zooming in to the area by holding *Cmd* and + can help. Now switch the Range to *Midtone* and, adjusting the brush size and *Exposure* as necessary, work on lightening the grey areas.

8 DARKEN LIGHT AREAS Repeat step 7 with the Burn Tool, found underneath the Dodge Tool in the toolbar. Set a low *Exposure*, select a soft, large brush and *Midtone* for your *Range*. Focus on the shadow areas and the darker mid-tones, increasing contrast by getting rid of as much grey as possible, without losing any detail, and boosting the blacks. If done right, this step can make the clouds look particularly dramatic.

Convert colour to mono infrared

You no longer need to have your DSLR converted to infrared to create mono infrared results. Using Photoshop, you can transform your images to add mono IR magic!

CONVERTING A SPARE DSLR to shoot infrared images can be costly – that's if you have a spare camera lying around, which few of us do. There are cheaper alternatives, such as filters that block visible light while only letting infrared light through to the sensor. But as these filters are opaque, it's virtually impossible to see through, which makes it difficult therefore to compose your shot. Now, thanks to our top technique, there is an easy way to achieve the mono infrared effect from a colour image: you can simulate for free, via a few steps in Photoshop, or by applying a plug-in filter from the likes of Nik Software.

Those shooting on an infrared-converted DSLR end up with a Raw file image that exhibits a pink cast, which requires some post-processing to convert it into the ethereal black & white image that has made it such a popular technique.

The creative effect works particularly well with landscape scenes that have lots of green foliage, as the green turns white, creating great contrast. Blue skies also add impact as they turn dark, making any clouds look dramatic. You can get some very interesting results if the photograph already has milky water from a long exposure too, adding to the ethereal quality of the infrared, like the image we're using for this step-by-step by professional photographer Adam Burton. It has vibrant green foliage, which should turn stark white once the effect has been applied, and a good tonal range that ensures we'll have a strong ratio of blacks and whites.

✅ Convert your DSLR
If you want to convert a camera so that it only captures infrared light, we'd recommend ACS in Norfolk due to their expertise in this area. Visit: www.advancedcameraservices.co.uk

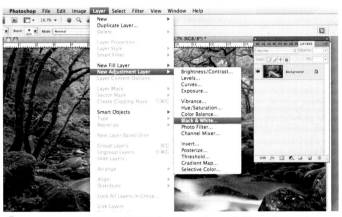

1 CONVERT TO BLACK & WHITE Open your image in Photoshop and go to *Layer>New Adjustment Layer>Black & White...* to convert your image to monochrome. This should then open an Adjustment Layer dialogue box, if not, double-click on the thumbnail in the Layers palette.

2 APPLY THE INFRARED FILTER You can apply an infrared effect by moving the sliders to modify the colours in the black & white image. You can do this manually using the *Yellow, Green* and *Blue* sliders or start with the *Infrared* filter, located via the *Preset* drop-down menu.

3 REFINE THE EFFECT While the filter does a pretty good job, it's just a starting point. Use the sliders to improve the effect further if you think it needs it. Here we adjusted the *Blue* slider slightly to pop the whites in the water. Be careful that you don't overdo it though and burn out the highlights, creating hotspots where you lose too much detail.

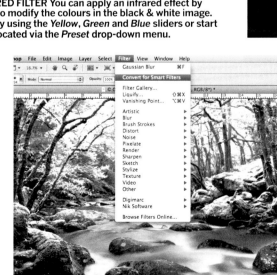

4 CREATE A SMART LAYER Next create an adjusted layer by holding down the *Alt* (Mac) or *Option* (PC) key and select *Layer>Merge Visible* to create a black & white version of your image. Now convert the layer to a Smart Filter by clicking on the layer and going to *Filter>Convert to Smart Filter*. This way you can edit any filter you apply after you commit to it.

Use Diffuse Glow
To really make your whites pop, you could try applying a small amount of the Diffuse Glow filter (*Filter>Distort>Diffuse Glow*) but don't overdo it and lose too much detail

Final image
The blur and popping whites has given a standard colour image an eye-catching and ethereal look of a fine-art infrared photograph.

5 BLUR THE IMAGE A true infrared image has luminous whites. To replicate a similar effect, apply Gaussian Blur. With the Smart Filter layer selected, go to *Filter>Blur>Gaussian Blur*. Go heavy on the blur – we set a Radius of 27.0 pixels – as you can always lower the layer's opacity later by moving the relevant slider at the top of the Layers palette.

6 ADJUST THE TONALITY Next, change the layer's blend mode (located in a drop-down menu at the top of the Layers palette) to *Overlay*, so the top layer interacts with the layer below it to boost contrast. If you need to bring some detail back to the shadows, go to *Image>Adjustments>Shadows/Highlights* and adjust the sliders as needed.

KIT FOR LANDSCAPES

Landscape photographers are a dedicated bunch ready to battle the elements for great images. If you're heading into the great outdoors, our guide ensures you've packed all the key essentials

LANDSCAPE PHOTOGRAPHY is easy, right? You just sling a camera over your shoulder, head into the countryside and great images will be staring you in the face. If only it were that simple! The reality is ridiculously early starts to catch the first light of the day, late finishes to shoot the sunset, routinely being battered by bad weather and tackling long walks shouldering heavy packs with the gnawing knowledge that it may all be for nothing if the light doesn't play ball.

But despite the setbacks, landscapes continue to be one of the most popular subjects to photograph, simply because when things do go to plan you could be moments away from taking the best photographs of your life. To do that, though, you do need the right gear – and we've got brilliant suggestions right here, whether you're a novice, enthusiast or semi-pro/pro.

Enthusiast p142

Semi-pro p144

Do not forget to pack ...

■ Waterproof cover: Protects your kit if you get caught in a sudden downpour. They're inexpensive and available from most camping shops.

■ Mini groundsheet: A square of polythene or a bin liner. Make that two – so you can keep your knees and bag dry when they're placed on wet ground.

■ Microfibre cloths: Pack several cloths to keep lenses and filters clean. Put them in plastic bags to keep them free of debris that could scratch delicate surfaces.

■ Maps and compass: Handy tools for knowing your location and establishing where the sun will rise and/or set. You can also buy apps for your smartphone.

■ Spirit level: Helps keep the camera level when it's mounted on a tripod, so you don't get a wonky horizon in your shots. Some cameras offer an electronic level.

■ Snacks & drinks: Pack high-energy snacks (energy bars, peanuts and chocolate are ideal) and drinks to keep you going. Please don't litter the countryside!

■ Air blower: Use it to remove sensor dust if necessary. Visible Dust, Giottos and GreenClean are all specialists with a range of products.

■ Bug spray: Heading to Scotland between May and September? Take spray to keep midges at bay. You'll find bug spray at Boots and other pharmacies.

■ Camera straps: Upgrade to a neoprene strap for added comfort. Our favourites are by Op/Tech, but several brands offer a choice of colours and styles.

Contacts

Arctic Butterfly
www.visibledust.com

B+W
www.daymen.co.uk

Canon
www.canon.co.uk

Cokin
www.intro2020.com

Depssi
www.bluepondimages.com

Gitzo
www.gitzo.co.uk

Giottos
www.daymen.co.uk

Green Clean
www.flaghead.co.uk

Hama
www.hama.co.uk

Hahnel
www.hahnel.ie

Hitech
www.formatt.co.uk

Hoodman
www.newprouk.co.uk

Jessops
www.jessops.com

Lowepro
www.daymen.co.uk

Lee Filters
www.leefilters.com

Manfrotto
www.manfrotto.co.uk

Nikon
www.nikon.co.uk

Op/Tech
www.newprouk.co.uk

Paramo
www.paramo.co.uk

Really Right Stuff
www.reallyrightstuff.com

Sprayway
www.sprayway.com

Sigma
www.sigma-imaging-uk.com

Slik
www.intro2020.com

Sony
www.sony.co.uk

Tamrac
www.intro2020.com

Tamron
www.intro2020.com

ThinkTank
www.snapperstuff.com

Velbon
www.intro2020.com

1) The landscape novice

So you fancy yourself as the next Joe Cornish or David Noton? You're probably drawn to the landscape by a general love of the great outdoors but have never taken more than snapshots while out on walks or enjoying other pursuits. Now you've added photography to your list of other hobbies it's time to up the ante. Here's a rundown of what you'll need to do just that...

✔ FILTER SYSTEM

In terms of value, the Cokin P System is the best there is. The filters are 84mm wide so the holder is big enough to avoid vignetting on lenses as wide as 14mm on DSLRs with APS-C sized sensors (20-24mm on full-frame) and there are adaptor rings available for lenses with threads up to 82mm. The holder costs around £5 and adaptor rings are £11 each. Whichever brand you buy, make sure you invest in a circular polariser and a set of ND grads. Cokin's P164 Circular Polariser costs £90, while its ND grads cost around £22 each.

✔ SUPERZOOM

Focal lengths from moderate wide to telephoto will cater for all your landscape needs, and if you want to have an easy life and compact kit, this can be covered in a single 18-200mm or 18-250mm zoom (equivalent to 28-300/375mm in full-frame format). Nikon and Canon have superzooms that are worth checking out, but don't write off independents such as the £200 Sigma 18-200mm f/3.5-6.3 DC OS or £180 Tamron 18-200mm f/3.5-6.3 XR Di II.

✔ BACKPACK

You'll be working with a fairly small kit so there's no need to invest in a giant backpack. You could get away with a 'Zoomster' case for your SLR and lens, like the £43 Think Tank Photo Digital Holster 20, and a belt-mounted pouch or bumbag for your accessories. However, a backpack like the £50 Lowepro Fastpack 350 is ideal as it holds all your kit, plus there's a top section for snacks and spare clothes, a laptop pocket for maps, and mesh outer side pockets for bottles of water.

✔ ENTRY LEVEL APS-C DIGITAL SLR

There are no poor DSLRs or CSCs – even the least expensive models give you fantastic image quality – so don't worry if your budget won't stretch to a pro-spec model as you really don't need one. What you do need is a relatively compact and lightweight DSLR that you can carry around all day and not notice, that's quick and easy to use and has the features to let you gradually take more control as your knowledge and experience grows. Models to consider include the £420 14.2-megapixel Nikon D3100 and the £400 Canon EOS 1100D.

✔ MEMORY CARDS

You'll have to be quite shutter-happy to fill a 4GB card, even on a good day, so one in the camera should be more than enough – though it's worth carrying a spare 4GB card just in case you get carried away.

✔ REMOTE RELEASE

When your camera's mounted on a tripod, firing the shutter with your finger can cause shake. Avoid it with a remote release that plugs into a socket on the side of your camera. Go for a basic model from Hama or Hähnel. The £25 Hähnel Remote Shutter Release is a great first remote to own.

✔ BASIC OUTDOOR CLOTHING

If you plan to be outdoors all day you need to make sure you're suitably dressed. The £25 Sprayway Explore Tee is a comfortable base layer, while the £68 Paramo Challenger is lightweight, reversible and offers excellent protection from wind and rain.

✔ TRIPOD

You may not like the idea of carrying a tripod around, but trust us, it is worth the effort – especially when shooting in low light at dawn or dusk. Better to use a tripod and low ISO for high image quality than hand-hold at high ISO. Go for a relatively lightweight model like the £90 Slik Pro 400DX or the £85 Jessops Major Carbon Fibre Tripod.

2) The advanced enthusiast

So you've been shooting seriously for two or three years now, you've picked up a lot of knowledge and experience along the way and your images are pretty good. Family and friends are asking you for prints for the wall and you're feeling pretty confident about your photography, so the time has come to upgrade your landscape kit. Here's what you might want to consider...

☑ REMOTE RELEASE

A decent remote release is a must. You could stick with a corded release, like the Hähnel 280 Remote Shutter Release shown on the previous page. However, you might also want to consider a wireless remote too, such as the £50 Hähnel Combi TF. As well as offering a four-second timer, it can be used in the studio to fire your flash system, making it a better choice if you also shoot portraits.

☑ ND GRAD FILTERS

When shooting landscapes, the sky is almost always brighter than the land so when you expose for the land, the sky blows out and looks horrible. The quickest and easiest way to avoid this is to pop an ND grad filter on your lens. A 0.6ND (two-stop) grad is fine for general use, while the 0.9ND (three-stop) grad is better at dawn and dusk. Cokin's Z-Pro ND grads cost £60 each, while Hitech's ND grads cost around £35 for its 100mm filters.

☑ FILTER SYSTEM

Although you could still get away with using a Cokin P-system holder with lenses as wide as 14mm, the fact that you've bought an ultra wide-angle zoom will probably be encouragement enough to go for a larger, 100mm system. Lee Filters will probably be over budget, but the Cokin Z-Pro system or Hitech 100mm system are more affordable. Holders cost around £50 each and adaptor rings are under £20 each.

☑ TRIPOD AND HEAD

Serious landscape photography means using a tripod all the time, so go for a well-made and sturdy model that's going to last, but isn't so big and heavy it's a chore to carry. The £260 Manfrotto 190CXPRO3 carbon-fibre is a worthy contender as is the £190 Giottos MTL8350B. If you're on a budget the £110 alloy Manfrotto 190XB is a fantastic buy. Pair this with a £75 Manfrotto 460MG head or £60 Giottos MH1302-652 ball head.

☑ BACKPACK

It's worth investing in a decent backpack that will take all your gear, offers a good degree of weather resistance and is comfortable to carry when walking long distances over rough ground. The £120 Lowepro Vertex 100AW is a great buy, as is the Tamrac £160 Expedition 7x and £135 Lowepro Pro Runner 450AW.

☑ TOP END APS-C DIGITAL SLR

You want the best that you can afford in APS-C format so that you can produce top quality images and print the files to 16x12in or bigger, without worrying about them looking unsharp or grainy. If you're already a Canon user, you're not going to better the £1,100 18-megapixel EOS 7D while for Nikon it has to be the £1,100 D300s or the £950 D7000. If you're starting from scratch, you should also consider the 16.2-megapixel £800 Sony Alpha A65.

☑ STANDARD ZOOM

If you've been using a kit zoom up to now, it's time to upgrade to a quality standard zoom. Focal lengths around 16mm are ideal for general use as they're wide enough to produce dramatic compositions. Around 35mm you'll get a similar angle-of-view and perspective to the human eye, while 50mm and beyond takes you into short telephoto territory. Check out the £600 Canon 15-85mm f/3.5-5.6 IS USM or £380 17-85mm f/4-5.6 IS USM, the £450 Nikkor AF-S 16-85mm f/3.5-5.6G ED VR, the £350 Sigma 17-70mm f/2.8-4 DC Macro OS HSM and the £340 Tamron 17-50mm f/2.8 XR Di II VC.

☑ SCREEN PROTECTOR

If you want your DSLR's monitor screen to do its job properly, it needs to be kept in good condition, so buy and fit a screen protector. The plastic clip-on variety available for some cameras are okay but are rather on the thick side and with a tendency to take on a 'frosted' look after a while. Self-adhesive protectors like the £6 protectors by Hama and Jessops are better options and also cheaper.

☑ PROTECTIVE CLOTHING

Comfort and protection is a must when your job involves being out in all weather shooting landscapes – if you get wet and cold you won't perform at your best and your work will suffer. Thankfully, technical outdoor clothing is better than ever so there's no excuse for getting caught out. In addition to wearing layers to trap heat and keep you warm, plus a hat to stop heat loss through your head, a breathable waterproof outer layer will protect you from both wind and rain. Regardless of whether you're a beginner, enthusiast or serious landscape photographer the need to stay dry and warm is the same. Brands to consider include Páramo, Berghaus, The North Face, Mountain Equipment and Mountain Hardwear, among others.

The £190 Velez Adventure Smock picture here offers one large kangaroo pocket, which can fit an OS map or filters. It's a short, comfortable waterproof top that's also light in weight. As with other Páramo waterproofs, the Velez Adventure pumps away perspiration so that when you stop, you don't get cold as you don't have any liquid close to your skin cooling you down.

While a pair of jeans are ideal for everyday use, they're not a good choice when you're spending a day out shooting as they're not weatherproof and will become clammy and heavy should you get caught in a shower. You are far better off wearing rainpants, which are comfortable, durable and above all waterproof. Shown here are the £40 Sprayway Havanna, which offer a decent budget option.

In the bag...

1) ULTRA WIDE-ANGLE ZOOM

Though you still tend to reach for your standard zoom first, it's worth adding an ultra wide-angle zoom to your kit as well so you can start to experiment with dramatic compositions, exploiting lines and foreground interest and creating images with a powerful sense of depth and scale. This is likely to become your 'standard' lens as you discover its benefits so make you buy a good one. The £500 Sigma 10-20mm f/3.5 EX DC HSM is possibly the best independent option, though the £650 Canon EF-S 10-22mm f/3.5-4.5 USM and the £660 Nikkor DX 10-24mm f/3.5-4.5 G AF-S are both contenders.

2) TELEZOOM

You won't use a telezoom as much but it's worth buying one for effects such as compression of perspective (great in misty weather), reduced depth-of-field and to allow you to fill the frame with details in the landscape. A 70-200mm is effectively a 105-300mm with APS-C sensors while a 70-300mm equates to 105-450mm, more than powerful enough. Check out the £300 Sigma 70-300mm f/4-5.6 DG OS, £170 Tamron 70-300mm f/4-5.6 DI LD Macro, £450 Nikkor AF-S 70-300mm f/4.5-5.6 VR and £500 Canon 70-200mm f/4L USM.

3) MEMORY CARDS

Though most shoots only last a day, you are venturing further afield and spending weekends on location, so you need extra cards. If you have four good days you could easily shoot 20-30GB of Raw files, so carry at least five 4GB cards.

4) HOOD LOUPE

Viewing images on your DSLR's preview screen can be tricky in bright light and though you can resort to pulling your jacket over the camera or cupping your hands, the best solution is the £80 Hoodman Loupe as it always gives a bright, distortion-free 1:1 view.

5) DEPSSI CARD

It only costs £2.99 but this handy accessory helps pinpoint the location of sunrise and sunset throughout the year – just align the card with True North and read off the indicator. Turn the card over and you've got a Hyperfocal distance chart that tells you where to focus your lens to maximise depth-of-field.

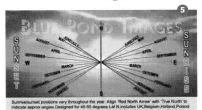

6) ND FILTERS

Use ND filters to increase exposures when shooting moving water and record that lovely blur effect. The Cokin Z-PRO NDs will set you back around £34 each and the ND4 and ND8 will be the most useful. Hitech's ND filters cost around £25 each.

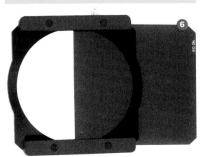

7) POLARISER

A polarising filter will deepen blue sky, reduce glare so colours appear richer, cut through haze and eliminate reflections. The £225 Cokin Z-PRO polariser is the ideal choice for use with the Z-PRO filter system, while Hitech's costs £130. If you can't stretch to a slot-in polariser, consider screw-in circular polarisers. Hoya offers an excellent range of polarisers, prices vary according to size, but expect to pay around £65 for a 72mm or 77mm filter.

3) The semi-pro/pro

Making a good full-time living from landscape photography is very difficult, but some manage it by diversifying – shooting stock images, selling prints, self-publishing cards and calendars, writing books and magazine articles and leading workshops. Semi-pros combine profitable photography with other ways of making money. Either way, if you fall into this category or want to, you're going to need gear that can withstand regular and sustained use in harsh conditions. Think of it as an investment in your future

☑ GLASS POLARISER

If you've invested in a Lee Filters kit you might as well complement it with a top quality polariser. The £220 105mm Lee circular polariser attaches to the Lee filter holder via an optional £33 105mm adaptor ring. However, the polariser has a deep mount so if you use ultra wide-angle zooms or lenses, consider a slimmer polariser, such as the £230 Heliopan Kasemann.

☑ ULTRA WIDE-ANGLE ZOOM

Focal lengths from 16-35mm on a full frame digital SLR are invaluable for landscape photography. An ultra wide-angle zoom is therefore likely to be your standard lens, so make sure you buy the best there is. From Canon there's the £1,160 16-35mm f/2.8L MkII USM and the £630 17-40mm f/4L USM. The latter offers very high image quality and costs half the price, while its slower maximum aperture isn't an issue for landscape photography. From Nikon the £1,320 AF-S 14-24mm f/2.8G ED has a good reputation. More practical is the £1,500 AF-S 17-35mm f/2.8D ED-IF, while the £850 AF-S 16-35mm f/4G ED VR is the first ultra wide-angle zoom with Vibration Reduction.

☑ FILTER SYSTEM

There's only one filter system that pro landscape photographers use: Lee Filters. It has no rival in terms of versatility and quality and though expensive – the basic holder is £55 and adaptor rings £19-55 – it's built to last. More importantly, the 100mm wide holder comes as a kit and can be set up with anything from one to three filter slots, allowing you to adapt it for use with wide-angle lenses. Fit two slots and you'll get vignette-free images with focal lengths as wide as 16mm on a full frame DSLR. There's also a SW150 system for use with the Nikkor 14-24mm and other ultra wide-angle zooms that have a protruding front element.

☑ TRIPOD HEAD

Tripod legs are only as good as the head you attach to them so don't blow your entire budget on fancy pins. A good, solid head is the £160 Manfrotto 410 Junior Head – it's well made and ideal for both single shots and sequences for stitched panoramas. If you prefer ball heads, pros love Arca Swiss and Really Right Stuff.

☑ TRIPOD

A solid, sturdy tripod that will keep your heavy full frame DSLR/ zoom combo still in high winds is essential. Carbon-fibre is common now, with Gitzo being the most popular brand among pros. Check out the £540 GT2541. If you don't like the Gitzo's twist leg locks, consider the £300 Manfrotto 055CXPRO4, and if you're on a budget you can't beat the classic £150 Manfrotto 055XPROB alloy tripod – heavier than carbon fibre but as tough as old boots. The £250 Giottos MTL8361B is another great choice.

✔ FULL-FRAME DSLR

In pre-digital days, medium- and large-format film cameras were the weapons of choice among pros but now medium-format quality can be achieved using a full frame DSLR, so it has become standard issue. Image quality aside, top-end full-frame DSLRs also boast excellent build quality, including full weather-sealing, so they can cope with daily use in extreme weather conditions and not even flinch. Rain, snow, wind, sand, volcanic ash – you name it. The two main players are the £5,300 Canon EOS-1Dx and the £5,080 Nikon D3x. However, the £1,700 Canon EOS 5D MkII, £1,800 Nikon D700 and £2,000 Sony Alpha 900 will also give excellent image quality, but lack the build quality and weatherproofing.

✔ GLASS SCREEN PROTECTOR

The rear screen on your DSLR will come in for some punishment so protect it with a £25 Giottos Aegis Pro Glass screen protector. You won't know there's a screen protector there at all and you can clean it as often as you like, safe in the knowledge that the real screen beneath it is as good as new.

✔ REMOTE RELEASE

Although you can get away with using a basic remote release, being a pro you might want to splash out on something a bit fancier, like the £130 Canon TC-80N3 or £130 Nikon MC-36. Both can be pre-programmed to make long exposures – handy if you use a ten-stop ND filter or shoot sequences of images at set intervals, which is useful for star trail photography. A cheaper option is Hahnel's feature-packed £70 Giga T Pro II.

✔ ULTIMATE OUTDOOR CLOTHING

It's well worth investing in high quality waterproof clothing if you plan to regularly shoot outdoors. Shown here is Paramo's £300 Halcon jacket, which has nine pockets, including large pockets that can fit most filter systems (including Lee), with plenty of room for batteries, memory cards and other accessories. Also shown is the best-selling £115 Paramo Cascada trousers, which offer full weather protection and excellent comfort. You can further preserve body heat by wearing a woollen hat from brands such as Patagonia or Berghaus.

✔ SENSIBLE FOOTWEAR

When you spend hours on your feet and regularly walk miles over rough terrain – all in a day's work for a landscape pro – you need a decent pair of boots that are comfortable, warm and protective. Check out boots by The North Face, Asolo, Meindl, Berghaus and Solomon. When shooting on boggy terrain, near water or on beaches, a good pair of wellies is far more useful as they will keep your feet bone dry. Aigle and La Chameau are reputable brands.

✔ BACKPACK

Invest in a backpack that's big enough to house all your camera kit as well as have extra space for maps, food, water, spare clothes – and is weather resistant. Lowepro is the brand of choice among landscape pros and the best pack has to be the £145 Pro Runner 450AW. Styled like a traditional rucksack, it has loads of features including mesh side pockets, large front pocket, fully padded interior, laptop compartment and memory card pockets on the inside of its lid.

In the bag...

1) FAST STANDARD ZOOM

A zoom from moderate wide to short telephoto is a vital part of the pro landscaper's kit. Go for one with a fast f/2.8 maximum aperture so you get a bright viewfinder image. The £1,000 Canon EF 24-70mm f/2.8L USM or the £1,200 Nikkor AF-S 24-70mm f/2.8G ED are the two favourites, but also consider the £350 Sigma 17-70mm f/2.8-4 DC OS and £345 Tamron SP 17-50mm f/2.8 VC Di II lens.

2) TELEZOOM

Though it's likely to be your least-used lens, a telezoom is still worth having for compressing perspective and shooting details in a scene. If you're a Canon user you can save a lot of weight, bulk and cash by opting for the £950 70-200mm f/4 IS USM instead of the £1,900 f/2.8 version – you don't need the extra speed for landscapes. For Nikon consider the £1,650 AF-S 70-200mm f/2.8G ED VR II. We'd also highly recommend Sigma's £1,000 70-200mm f/2.8 EX DG OS HSM.

3) BACK-UP FULL-FRAME DSLR

If your budget will run to it, a second body is worth having just in case your main one decides to malfunction or you damage it on location. It needn't be as high-specced as your main body – if you normally use a Canon EOS-1Ds MkIII, for example, buy an EOS 5D MkII as back-up, or an £1,800 Nikon D700 alongside the D3x.

SPARE BATTERIES

Goes without saying really – nothing worse than running out of batteries in the middle of nowhere when the light's great. Always set out with two fully-charged batteries. As well as branded batteries, Delkin, Hama and Hahnel all offer alternatives.

4) MEMORY CARDS

Trips away can last a week or more and with you shooting every day from dawn to dusk when the weather plays ball, you'll soon start filling up your memory cards. Downloading full cards to a laptop is a daily routine, but if you prefer not to re-format cards until you're home, then carry at least 50GBs of capacity, in other words six or seven 8GB cards.

ND FILTERS

As well as your ten-stop ND filter, it's worth carrying a couple of weaker NDs so you can use slower shutter speeds when shooting waterfalls and rivers to capture motion. A polariser can be used like an ND filter as it loses two stops of light (equivalent to an ND 0.6), but also add ND 0.9 (three-stop) and maybe ND 1.2 (four-stop) as well so you have more options. Lee Filters ProGlass NDs cost around £110 each.

5) TEN-STOP ND FILTER

No self-respecting pro would be without one. Go for the £130 Lee Big Stopper or the B+W 3.0ND screw-in filter. Prices vary depending on the filter size, for example a 52mm filters costs around £41 while a 77mm costs £130.

6) ND GRADS

The most useful filters of all for landscape photography are Neutral Density (ND) grads as they allow you to produce a well-exposed landscape and a well-exposed sky in one shot, in-camera. Invest in a £200 ND grad set from Lee Filters, which contains 0.3, 0.6 and 0.9 density grads, and go for the Hard grads rather than Soft grads as they're more effective and easier to use.

PIECE OF CARD

A sheet of 10x8in stout card is handy to use as a lens shade when shooting in strong sunlight, to shield the front end of the lens and prevent flare. A lens hood would do that, but when using a filter holder, the hood that came with the lens obviously won't fit!

7) SENSOR CLEANING KIT

You may not want to carry it in your backpack, but keep a kit in your car. It's worth having access to a decent sensor cleaning kit in case you need it, such as the £75 Arctic Butterfly 788 Brite sensor brush.

8) APPLE IPHONE 4 OR 4S

Not only invaluable for keeping in touch, and taking decent photos with its five-megapixel camera, the Apple iPhone 4 is a powerhouse of technology. For example, if you take reference shots using the camera you can pinpoint their location on Google Maps by tapping the Places option in the Camera Roll. The Apple iPhone's GPS capability lets you know exactly where your landscape shots are taken, so you can find your way back to the same spot – or share the information with others. You can also download the app: The Photographer's Ephemeris (http://photoephemeris.com), which allows you to establish the time and direction of sunrise and sunset anywhere in the world.

Wide-angle lenses

If you're serious about landscape photography, the first addition you should invest in is a decent wide-angle lens. The exaggerated perspective and wide angle-of-view that these lenses gives allows you to fill the frame with your scene and reveal an incredible amount of detail. When you're confronted by a beautiful landscape, there is nothing like a wide-angle lens to ensure the whole scene is recorded, from foreground interest through to distant subjects. Experienced landscape photographers have learned how to use the way that wide-angle lenses stretch perspective to their advantage to give images with strong foreground interest and incredible depth. Another reason why wide-angles are wonderful choices for landscapes is because they have an apparent abundance of depth-of-field, even at mid-aperture settings, to produce images with an excellent amount of sharpness. So, now you're sold on wide-angle lenses, you'll need to decide which type is best for you.

Understanding focal lengths: Wide-angles

The focal length stated on a lens relates to SLRs using 35mm film and full-frame sensors. If your camera has an APS-C-sized sensor (most have), then you're effectively cropping the image and increasing the focal length of the lens (by 1.5x with Nikon, Pentax and Sony; 1.6x with Canon). The chart below shows popular wide-angles and the change in effective focal length.

Focal length on lens	Sensor size Full-frame	APS-H	APS-C	APS-C (Canon)	Four-Thirds & Micro Four-Thirds
	1x	**1.3x**	**1.5x**	**1.6x**	**2x**
8mm	8mm	10mm	12mm	13mm	16mm
14mm	14mm	18mm	21mm	22mm	28mm
15mm	15mm	19mm	22mm	23mm	30mm
20mm	20mm	26mm	30mm	32mm	40mm
24mm	24mm	31mm	36mm	38mm	48mm
28mm	28mm	36mm	42mm	45mm	56mm
10-17mm	10-17mm	13-22mm	15-25mm	16-27mm	20-34mm
10-20mm	10-20mm	13-26mm	15-30mm	16-32mm	20-40mm
10-22mm	10-22mm	13-29mm	15-33mm	16-35mm	20-44mm
11-18mm	11-18mm	14-23mm	16-27mm	18-29mm	22-36mm
12-24mm	12-24mm	16-31mm	18-36mm	19-38mm	24-48mm
16-35mm	16-35mm	21-45mm	24-53mm	26-56mm	32-70mm
17-35mm	17-35mm	22-45mm	25-53mm	27-56mm	34-70mm
17-40mm	17-40mm	22-52mm	25-60mm	27-56mm	34-80mm

Make the most of wide-angle lenses

Shooting wide will ensure your shots are full of detail and impact. Here's why...

WIDE-ANGLES ARE the lens of choice for the vast majority of landscape photographers and for very good reason. These lenses allow you to squeeze as much of a location into your viewfinder as possible and capture a scene absolutely brimming with detail and interest.

This is an advantage for landscape photographers as it means you can include foreground interest as well as lots of detail in the scene beyond, giving your image depth. By choosing interesting foreground subject matter, you can also grab the viewer's attention and pull them in to the picture.

Using wide-angle zooms can be so addictive that you automatically use their widest setting at every opportunity. But this can pose problems. Some lenses can be set so wide that they show the corners of your equipment (lenses, filters and holders) in the frame; this is known as vignetting. Another issue with using extreme wide-angle lenses is barrel distortion, which causes horizons to bend and buildings to lean.

All this can be avoided by training yourself to set your wide-angle lens according to your subject matter. If shooting a straight horizon, like a seascape, then using the focal length a few millimetres up from the widest will reduce the appearance of a bendy horizon. A mountainous terrain, which already has an uneven horizon, can be shot as wide as you want. As well as focal length, pay attention to the height and the angle of your camera when you set it up on a tripod. Trees will lean when composed from low to the ground, so try setting the camera at head height and you may notice a big difference.

The benefits of shooting with wide-angle lenses far outweigh these few considerations. The impact they can give on your photographs is astounding, which is why it comes as no surprise that most pro landscape photographers wouldn't shoot without them.

Format

Vignetting

Low viewpoint

ABOVE: CHOOSE A FORMAT
My first image was taken in a horizontal format, which is often the natural orientation for landscapes. However, a vertical format can work just as well with wide-angle shots. It allows more room for foreground details while still including lots of sky.

FAR LEFT: DON'T GO TOO WIDE
Using the widest end of your zoom may mean your images suffer from barrel distortion and vignetting. Barrel distortion is when the horizon curves downwards. When dark areas appear in the corners of your frame, you are suffering from a spot of vignetting. The wider your focal length, the greater the chance the camera has of including parts of your kit (eg filter holders). Avoid both problems by not setting your lens to its widest focal length.

LEFT: GO LOW A viewpoint closer to the ground dramatically increases the impact of the foreground subject matter and provides a more dynamic composition. Now the viewer can focus their attention on the rock pool, which leads their eye into the frame and towards the distant castle.

Final image

Wide-angle landscapes are most effective when there's some prominent foreground interest to pull the viewer in to the scene. Don't be afraid to compose so that your foreground is big and bold!

Choosing a wide-angle

You've a choice of several outstanding options

IF YOUR CAMERA was supplied with a 'standard' zoom kit lens, such as an 18-55mm, then you'll already have a lens capable of shooting wide-angle images. However, its capabilities are restricted, as its field-of-view is not wide enough to really make the most of landscape photography, so while good enough choice to get you started, you should add a better wide-angle at your first opportunity. Your two main options are a fixed wide-angle lens or a wide-angle zoom. If you want the absolute sharpest possible results, then in theory you want a prime lens, with a 15mm the best choice for APS-C sensors or a 20mm or 24mm for a full frame model. While marque lenses offer the ultimate optical performance, they're expensive and your choice is limited. If your camera has the smaller APS-C sized sensor, we'd strongly recommend that you opt for an ultra wide-angle zoom: they're relatively affordable, you have far more choice and they deliver excellent quality.

The arrival of DSLRs has seen high-quality ultra-wide zooms become increasingly popular. That's no surprise as they offer incredible versatility in such a small and inexpensive lens. In fact, the ultra wide-angle zoom is arguably one of the best value lenses you could own. There is a variety of focal lengths available, with those around 11-22mm being the most suitable for use with an APS-C sized sensor. In truth, all cover a very similar range, although there are one or two exceptions to note. The Pentax 10-17mm fisheye offers a 180° angle-of-view at its widest end, so in a sense you're getting a fisheye and ultra-wide zoom rolled into one. It's also worth noting that unlike most ultra-wide zooms, the Sigma 12-24mm can be used on full frame and APS-C DSLRs. Finally, while 16-35mm zooms are popular with full frame DSLR users, the effective focal length of 24-53mm (26-56mm on a Canon) is limited for APS-C.

So which wide-angle lens should you buy? There's little doubt that zooms represent superb value for money and you're spoilt for choice as there aren't any poor performers in this category. Here we recommend our favourite lenses, all of which will deliver great results. While primes offer the ultimate in quality, zooms are better value and deliver excellent results. We've stated average street prices at time of publication.

DIGITAL-ONLY LENSES
When you're choosing a lens, check to see if it's for use with film and digital SLRs, or for DSLRs only. Those made for film and digital are usually more expensive; those designed exclusively for DSLRs are optically optimised for digital. Therefore, if you're using a DSLR with an APS-C sensor and never plan to buy a full frame DSLR, go for a digital-only lens.

Fixed or zoom lens?

It's the age-old question – why buy a fixed lens with only one focal length when a zoom offers so much more versatility? Well, here's why...

FIXED ('PRIME') WIDE-ANGLE LENS
✔ Simpler optical design generally means sharper results with better contrast
✔ Fast maximum aperture gives brighter viewfinder and better low-light capabilities
✔ Smaller and more compact than a zoom
✔ Most have a smaller filter thread
✘ Limited to one focal length
✘ Relatively expensive

WIDE-ANGLE ZOOM LENS
✔ Covers several focal lengths, so you're spoilt for wide-angle versatility
✔ At its wide end, it offers far better coverage than a fixed lens
✔ Most zooms are optically excellent
✔ Lots of flexibility at a very good price
✘ Not as sharp as a fixed lens, especially towards the edges and corners of the frame
✘ Suffers from more distortion
✘ Maximum aperture isn't as fast as fixed lens
✘ Most have a larger filter thread, so screw-in filters are more expensive

Wide-angle anatomy

1) PETAL HOOD
Ultra wide-angles come supplied with a dedicated hood to avoid vignetting and flare.

2) LARGE, CONCAVE FRONT ELEMENT The front element normally has a prominent curve, leaving it exposed to dust and scratches, so take care to keep it clean.

3) MANUAL FOCUS RING
Normally towards the front of the lens and reasonably wide. You'll rarely need to use it, as wide-angle lenses have excellent AF.

4) ZOOM RING These are normally found towards the back of the barrel. Most are wide with a grooved surface to allow you to grip it easily.

5) FOCUS DISTANCE
Many lenses have the focus distance scale marked on the barrel, while some of the more upmarket models have a focus distance window.

6) HYPERFOCAL SCALE
(see inset) This scale allows you to estimate how much of the scene will appear sharp thanks to the depth-of-field created by the choice of aperture that you set.

7) INTERNAL FOCUSING SYSTEM
If you're planning to use filters, lenses with an internal focusing system offer the benefit that the front of the lens doesn't rotate when focusing, so you don't have to keep readjusting them.

Zeiss 21mm f/2.8 Distagon

LENS CONSTRUCTION:
16 elements in 13 groups
APERTURE RANGE: f/2.8 to f/22
FILTER THREAD: 82mm
DIMENSIONS: 87x109mm
WEIGHT: 600g
FITTINGS: Canon, Nikon and Pentax
WEBSITE: www.robertwhite.co.uk
This is an almost legendary lens for connoisseurs that's available in Canon, Nikon and Pentax fittings. It is manual focus only, with a smooth focusing action and it uses a manual aperture ring.

The depth-of-field scale is clear and allows for accurate depth-of-field calculations. This is an expensive lens but boasts an exceptional optical performance, resolving an amazing amount of detail. It's absolutely the ultimate choice for quality.

£1,500

Canon 24mm f/1.4L II USM

LENS CONSTRUCTION:
13 elements in ten groups
APERTURE RANGE: f/1.4 to f/22
FILTER THREAD: 77mm
DIMENSIONS: 93.5 x 86.9mm
WEIGHT: 650g
FITTINGS: Canon only
WEBSITE: www.canon.co.uk
This recent addition to the Canon range is designed for pro use, as its price tag suggests. As well as offering an extremely fast aperture, it boasts weather and dust seals to protect it from the elements. Optical quality is superb, thanks to the aspherical and UD glass elements, which ensure image sharpness is crisp throughout the frame. A dream lens for those that can afford it, but the Zeiss 21mm f/2.8 Distagon, while manual focus, offers a superior optical performance to the Canon.

£1,350

Nikon AF-SDX12-24mmf/4ED-IF

LENS CONSTRUCTION:
11 elements in seven groups
APERTURE RANGE: f/4 to f/22
FILTER THREAD: 77mm
DIMENSIONS: 82.5 x 90mm
WEIGHT: 485g
FITTINGS: Nikon only
WEBSITE: www.nikon.co.uk

This excellent zoom, for DSLRs with APS-C-sensors only, is compact considering the f/4 maximum aperture. It's partly made of plastic but feels well made. The zoom ring is wide and the focusing ring is adequate with both offering a smooth action. The barrel sports a focusing window and internal focusing. Image quality is very high, delivering very sharp results throughout the range. Chromatic aberration and flare is barely noticeable but slight barrel distortion is evident.

£800

Canon EF17-40mmf/4LUSM

LENS CONSTRUCTION:
12 elements in nine groups
APERTURE RANGE: f/4 to f/22
FILTER THREAD: 77mm
DIMENSIONS: 83.5 x 96.8mm
WEIGHT: 475g
FITTINGS: Canon only
WEBSITE: www.canon.co.uk

The Canon L-series lenses offer higher than normal performance, so this zoom, with its constant f/4 aperture, is one of the most popular optics in the Canon stable. Suitable for use with all EOS models, it's larger than most but robustly built, with great handling and fast AF. Optics are excellent, although with full-frame sensors edge detail becomes a little soft. It's a great lens, although the EF-S 10-22mm is a better choice for those with DSLRs boasting an APS-C sensor.

£620

Sigma 10-20mmf/4-5.6EXDCHSM

LENS CONSTRUCTION:
14 elements in ten groups
APERTURE RANGE: f/1.8 to f/22
FILTER THREAD: 77mm
DIMENSIONS: 83.5 x 81mm
WEIGHT: 470g
FITTINGS: Canon, Nikon, Pentax, Sigma and Sony
WEBSITE:
www.sigma-imaging-uk.com

A real favourite with landscape lovers thanks to its compact design and sharp optics. Like all Sigma EX lenses, it's very nicely put together and it feels and looks the part. The barrel sports wide zoom and manual focus rings, both of which have a smooth action. Optics deliver high sharpness and only slight evidence of distortion or aberration. It's a better choice than the newer f/3.5 version.

£430

Sigma 8-16mmf/4.5-5.6DCHSM

LENS CONSTRUCTION:
15 elements in 11 groups
APERTURE: f/4.5-5.6 to f/22
FILTER THREAD: None
DIMENSIONS: 75x105.7mm
WEIGHT: 545g
FITTINGS: Canon, Nikon, Pentax, Sigma & Sony
WEBSITE:
www.sigma-imaging-uk.com

With an effective focal length of 12-24mm (12.8-25.6mm on a Canon), the Sigma provides wide-angle opportunities not previously available for APS-C DSLRs. Build quality is excellent and AF is fast and responsive. Its most impressive aspect is the optics. It boasts four elements in FLD ('F' Low Dispersion) glass and three aspherical elements and delivers very sharp results. A versatile, high quality zoom.

£550

Voigtlander 20mmf/3.5ColorSkoparSLII

LENS CONSTRUCTION:
Nine elements in six groups
APERTURE RANGE: f/3.5 to f/22
FILTER THREAD: 52mm
DIMENSIONS: 63x28.8mm
WEIGHT: 205g
FITTINGS: Nikon and Pentax
WEBSITE: www.robertwhite.co.uk

This is one of the most affordable prime lenses on the market and also one of the smallest and lightest, as well as being manual focus only. This last point generally isn't an issue for landscape photographers. The manual focus action is smooth and the barrel boasts a clear hyperfocal scale that makes achieving a good depth-of-field a breeze, as well as an aperture ring. Optically, this lens is a very good performer with excellent sharpness once stopped down. A great budget prime lens.

£505

Tamron 10-24mmf/3.5-4.5DiIILD

LENS CONSTRUCTION:
12 elements in nine groups
APERTURE RANGE: f/3.5-4.5 to f/22
FILTER THREAD: 77mm
DIMENSIONS: 83.2 x 86.5mm
WEIGHT: 406g
FITTINGS: Canon, Nikon, Pentax and Sony
WEBSITE: www.intro2020.co.uk

Tamron's 11-18mm zoom has been a popular choice for years but this recent addition, with its extremely wide focal length range, brings even more versatility to wide-angle fans. It's a compact and lightweight option with good handling and an internal focusing system that will please filter users. Optical quality is very good, thanks to the inclusion of aspherical and LD (Low Dispersion) elements and enhanced multi-coatings.

£365

Telephoto zooms

THERE IS NO ARGUMENT that landscape photographers should place a decent wide-angle lens (be it prime or zoom) at the top of their wishlist. However, that's not to say there shouldn't be a little room allocated in the gadget bag for a telezoom. While you'll predominantly be filling the frame with wide-angle vistas, you'll also find times when a telephoto can prove useful. This will usually be when you want to isolate a specific area or feature within the scene or when you want to create a layering effect through perspective compression (see below). There are a variety of telephoto zooms available but we'd recommend you opt for a focal length of around 55-200mm if you use a DSLR with an APS-C sized sensor, or a 70-300mm or similar zoom if you have a full-frame DSLR. You'll find the Tamron 55-200mm f/4-5.6 DiII to be great value, along with Sigma's 70-300mm f/4-5.6 DG zoom. Both of these will be perfect for filling the frame with any wildlife you may encounter as you roam the countryside.

Perspective compression

Photographers often talk about using a telephoto to compress perspective, but what does it mean?

TECHNICALLY SPEAKING, telephoto lenses don't 'compress perspective', but, practically speaking, you do get a different feeling of perspective from a telephoto shot than from a scene captured with a wide-angle lens. Wide-angle lenses open up perspective and create a sense of depth because nearby objects appear big, and further objects appear to be small, suggesting distance. Add to this that wide-angle lenses create strong diagonals, enhancing the sense of depth. On the other hand, telephotos make distant objects appear larger, apparently compressing the planes of the image and reducing the impression of depth. Lines tend not to stretch into diagonals and parallels remain parallel, increasing the two-dimensional feel. Compared to a wide-angle view, this all adds up to an image that is more static. And, of course, the longer the lens, the greater the effect. So what kind of images benefit from the compression effects of longer lenses? The static character of telephoto images suits tranquil scenes; hilly landscapes are ideal, especially where there are several planes or 'layers' that can be visually pulled together so they appear to be almost stacked on top of each other. The feeling of tranquility can be enhanced by early morning mist, with the tops of the hills rising above a sea of mist. More dramatic images can be created in the right lighting conditions – look for alternating bands of light and dark, creating a 'layering of light'. Urban landscapes also work well as you can use compression to juxtapose elements or suggest a crowded environment.

28mm

50mm

75mm

28-35mm

The apparent distance between the foreground and castle creates a sense of depth, with the hills and village behind the castle stretching away into the distance.

60-85mm

Even at moderate telephoto settings, the perspective seems much flatter, and the castle seems to loom over the distant hills and the village.

105-200mm

As the focal length increases, perspective seems to flatten out, so that the castle and the hills behind seem to be almost in the same plane.

120mm

200mm

Landscapes filters: Systems and types

Filters have long been the simplest and most inexpensive way to improve or alter your images in-camera. Even in the digital age, they have their place in every landscape photographer's kit bag. We explain the main types of filter systems, our recommended filter types and the major brands to consider...

THE WORTH OF FILTERS, now that we have Photoshop, is a topic that still divides opinion amongst amateur photographers. But for those that like to get it right in-camera, filters are still invaluable tools, in particular with outdoor photographers.

While some filters can give an image a colour cast, other popular types are neutral in tone and instead enable photographers to balance bright and dark areas of a scene, or have more scope for their choice of apertures and shutter speeds. There are many different uses for filters to suit all types of photography but in this guide, we help you decide which type of filter, as well as what filter system, is the best choice for landscape photography.

Filters come in two main types: screw-in, which attach directly to the filter thread at the front of your lens barrel; and slot-in, which slip into a holder held in place on the front of your lens by adapter rings screwed on to the filter thread. Both have their pros and cons, which you should consider before deciding which to buy. As you'll no doubt discover as you read on, a combination of both types is often the best solution for most photographers.

▦ Screw-in filters

These are quick and easy to attach and remove from your lens, so are a very convenient choice. As they're made from glass, they are of high optical quality and more difficult to scratch. Screw-in filters come in various sizes, with 52mm to 77mm being the most common. If you own a number of lenses, each with different filter threads, you will either need a filter in each size or take the more affordable option of a stepping ring (see tip below).

Another negative point worth considering is that grad filters aren't well suited for use as a screw-in, which will be off-putting for landscape photographers in particular. You also need to take care when using more than one screw-in filter at a time, as you run the risk of vignetting (darkening at the image corners), especially with wide-angle lenses. Another disadvantage is that occasionally you may find a filter won't budge, in which case you'll need a filter clamp to help remove it.

Top tip: Stepping rings

A cheaper option than buying the same type of filter in various sizes is to buy the largest size you need and a step-down ring, which allows you to fit a large filter on a smaller thread. For instance, if you have a 72mm filter and buy a 72-67 ring, you can screw the filter to the ring, which attaches easily to the lens. Don't go for a step-up ring for attaching smaller filters to larger lenses, as these can cause vignetting.

▦ Slot-in filters

With these systems, you only need to buy one filter even if you have several lenses of different sizes. This is because the filter slips into a holder, which attaches to the lens via an adapter ring. So, instead of needing costly screw-ins in various sizes, you can simply buy affordable adapter rings in the sizes you need and swap the holder between them. It does mean the initial investment is higher but over time, it proves to be a far more economical, especially if you have several lenses.

You'll find there are an extensive range of filters available, in particular graduates, which are among the most popular types of filter for landscapes. Unlike screw-in filters, slot-in filters are made from optical resin, which is incredibly tough and lighter than glass, although more prone to scratches. Optically, they offer excellent quality, with little discernible quality to screw-ins. For the ultimate quality, look at pro-brands like Lee Filters, which use the very best materials.

Top tip: Compatibility

You'll find most brands make more than one size of slot-in system to suit different types of DSLRs. The standard size is 67mm but if you have wide-angle lenses, we'd recommend you consider the 85mm or 100mm formats. Note that as these sizes are standard, similarly sized holders will accept filters from other brands.

Our favourite filter types

There are literally hundreds of different types of filter available, but our shortlist below highlights those that will prove most beneficial to your photography

Skylight/UV/ Protection filters

These are essentially clear glass filters that protect the front element of your lens from dust, marks and damage. The UV filter also aids in the removal of haze but all three are more or less the same. We'd recommend you attach one to each of your lenses.

Close-up filters

On bright days when the sun is high in the sky and not particularly suitable for landscape photography, many photographers turn their attention to shooting details in the scenery. Close-up filters are useful if you don't own a macro lens and want to shoot small objects at high magnification.

No filter

ND filter

Neutral Density

These aren't essential filters, but are very useful. A Neutral Density filter is grey in colour and doesn't alter the colour balance of an image but instead reduces the amount of light passing through to the lens. They are mainly used in bright sunlight, when you need to use a wide aperture to minimise depth-of-field, or a slower shutter speed to emphasise movement.

Polariser

If you shoot outdoors regularly, buy a polarising filter. It saturates colours, in particular blue sky, as well as minimising glare and reflections from shiny surfaces like foliage or water. The effect of a polariser can't be replicated accurately in Photoshop, which is why most landscape photographers never leave home without one. Avoid linear polarisers – you need a circular polariser; otherwise your camera won't meter correctly. Polarisers have a filter factor of 4x and reduces the exposure by two stops, so watch out for camera shake. While one of the most expensive types of filter, they're definitely worth the investment.

No grad

0.9ND grad

ND Graduate filter

Graduates have a dark area that fades to clear and are used to balance bright sky with a darker foreground. They're available in a variety of colours, but we'd say the only grad to buy at first is the ND (Neutral Density) graduate. These have a gradual ND effect that does not change the colour balance of the sky, but allows detail to be recorded in the scene. ND grads are available in various densities, with the 0.6ND grad being a good first choice. You'll find that there are soft- or hard-edged variants too, relating to how the grad effect falls off – we'd suggest you begin with a soft-edged grad.

ND filter factors: This table explains the relationship between exposures and filter factors. Light loss is stated in stops.

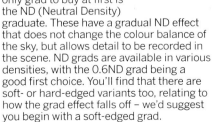

Density	Filter factor	Light loss
0.3	2x	1
0.6	4x	2
0.9	8x	3
1.2	16x	4

Using slot-in filters

1) Screw in the appropriate adapter ring
2) Attach the holder to the ring
3) Slide the filter into the holder

Screw in filters

Guide prices for popular brands

	UV	Polariser	ND
B+W			
52mm	£32	£68	£22
55mm	£32	£77	£25
58mm	£35	£79	£25
62mm	£38	£83	£28
67mm	£45	£99	£35
72mm	£53	£114	£40
77mm	£70	£129	£55
Hoya			
52mm	£30	£45	£28
55mm	£35	£45	£32
58mm	£40	£45	£35
62mm	£45	£55	£38
67mm	£50	£55	£40
72mm	£55	£65	£58
77mm	£65	£65	£68
Jessops			
52mm	£20	£33	-
55mm	£20	£35	-
58mm	£20	£30	-
62mm	£28	£45	-
67mm	£28	£38	-
72mm	£38	£55	-
77mm	£38	£63	-
Kood			
52mm	£8	£18	£12
55mm	£8	£21	£13
58mm	£8	£22	£15
62mm	£9	£30	£15
67mm	£9	£30	£19
72mm	£10	£36	£28
77mm	£12	£38	£29
Tiffen			
52mm	£12	£30	£23
55mm	£12	£30	£25
58mm	£15	£35	£30
62mm	£15	£40	£30
67mm	£18	£45	£35
72mm	£25	£55	£50
77mm	£25	£60	£50

Filter brands

There aren't too many brands of filter but the choice they offer can be confusing. We've highlighted the tried and tested filter brands that offer great value as well as high-quality products

B+W

www.daymen.co.uk

THIS PRESTIGIOUS German brand is renowned for producing screw-in filters with optimum quality, both in terms of the metal filter ring and the manufacturing process behind its premium, optical glass. It's a very popular brand with pros but it does cost around twice as much as other brands. If you need the ultimate in quality from a screw-in filter, then B+W is the option for you, otherwise, Hoya is a great choice. One string in its bow is the ten-stop ND filter, which has proven incredibly popular for daytime long-exposure photography.

Hoya

www.intro2020.co.uk

HOYA PRODUCES around 60% of the world's optical glass, so you can be assured it offers excellent quality and value. Hoya offers the most extensive range of any screw-in filter system, with literally every type of filter you can imagine. What's more, for popular types of filter such as polariser or UV, it has a number of options to suit all levels of photographer from amateur through to pro. Its filters boast several cutting edge technologies, for instance the HD series boasts hardened glass and several layers of multi-coating to improve contrast and reduce flare, while the Pro 1 Digital series have been exclusively designed for use with digital cameras. The extensive Super HMC series covers the majority of filter types and provides fantastic quality at a great price. It's worth downloading Hoya's filter brochure to get a better idea of the full range of filters on offer.

Cokin

www.intro2020.co.uk

FOR MANY photographers over the decades, the search for high-quality and affordable slot-in filters started and ended with Cokin. This isn't a surprise, because this manufacturer was the innovator of creative filters for amateur photographers and has led the way ever since. Cokin offers four filter sizes as follows: 67mm (A-series); 84mm (P-series); 100mm (Z-Pro) and 130mm (X-Pro) . The A-series is aimed more for use with compacts or camcorders, so the P-series is the best introductory option. If you use wide-angle lenses with a focal length wider than 28mm, you should consider the Z-Pro range, while the X-Pro is more for medium-format photographers. All the ranges offer plenty of options but the P-series has everything the DSLR photographer may ever need, with over 140 filters to choose from, including polarisers and a variety of ND grads. Filter rings are available for threads up to 82mm and the P-holder accepts up to three filters at a time. The Z-Pro series is a better choice for landscape photographers in particular those with ultra-wide zooms. Adaptor rings are available from 49mm to 96mm and filters are 100mm square, except for the grads which are 100x150mm.

All the filters are made from CR39 optical resin and deliver high-quality results and because it's such a popular range, filters are very well priced. The ND Grad Kit for the P-series is affordable at £50 and consists of a Cokin P filter holder, one P121L ND2 Light Grad, one P121M ND4 Grad and one P121S ND8 Soft Grad filter. The Cokin P164 circular polariser is around £60 while for the Z-Pro, you're looking at around £225 for the Z164!

Adapter rings cost as follows: A-series: £8; P-series: £11; X-Pro: £50 and Z-Pro: £22.

Jessops

www.jessops.com

ITS RANGE of screw-in filters may be limited to 21 protection and polarising filters, but with prices starting at £20 for a 52mm Skylight or UV, it's a good place to start your filter collection. They're well made too, so you won't have to worry about quality. Most filters are kept in stock in-store as well as being available for home delivery.

Lee Filters

www.leefilters.com

LEE FILTERS is the ultimate choice for the discerning photographer. Loved by pros and relished by enthusiasts, Lee Filters are as good as it gets in terms of optical quality, but due to the stringent manufacturing processes involved, expect it to command high prices. Its brilliant 100mm system is the cornerstone of its success, with a high quality and versatile holder that can be made to your own specification to hold varying numbers of filters. The filters themselves are brilliant quality and are manufactured from a number of materials, including glass, resin and polyester. Various kits are available and we'd recommend the £200 Digital Starter kit, which comprises of an assembled holder, 0.6ND ProGlass ND hard grad, 0.6 ND and cleaning cloth, all packed neatly into a pouch. The other kit is the £150 Starter kit, which includes an assembled filter holder, 0.6ND grad, cleaning cloth, Coral 3 grad and pouch. Its ten-stop 'Big Stopper' ND (around £130) is the best on the market. Adaptor rings from 49mm to 77mm cost £19, 82mm and 86mm are £41 while 93mm, 95mm and 105mm rings are £55. The filter holder (the Foundation kit) is £55. If you intend making a living from photography and investing in expensive lenses, then these are the filters you should aspire to own.

Filter aid
Do not underestimate how filters can be used to improve your images, especially if you're keen on shooting landscapes.

Formatt (Hitech)

www.formatt.co.uk

FORMATT MAKES a range of filters for movies and stills photography. Its Hitech filters are aimed specifically at digital SLR photographers, made from optical resin and are manufactured in the UK to extremely high standards to provide excellent optical quality. The 67mm, 85mm and 100mm filter systems are compatible with other slot-in brands and include an extensive range of graduates. As well as hard- and soft-edged ND grads (from 0.3-1.2), it offers a huge choice of colour grads, as well as the Blender, which graduates the effect through the entire length of the filter. Hitech isn't as well known or as widely available as Cokin, but is a good alternative. An ND grad kit with 0.3, 0.6 and 0.9 ND grads costs £45 (85mm); £100 (100mm) and £130 (100x150mm). The circular polariser costs £133 (85mm) or £140 (100mm). A plastic holder costs under £10 and plastic adaptor rings costs around £5 from 49mm to 77mm.

Kood

www.kood-international.com

KOOD HAS its own range of filters, with screw-in filters imported from Japan and slot-in filters manufactured in the UK. The range of screw-in filters isn't too large but includes polarisers, protection and close-up filters, as well as various special effect items such as starburst and colour correction filters. Kood also has a good range of stepping rings too. Kood offers four sizes of slot-in filters: 67mm, 84mm, 100mm and 130mm, so its filters are compatible with all the major slot-in brands. Made from CR39 optical resin, they offer decent quality and are a good budget buy. Kood isn't available from all high-street outlets, so visit its website for your nearest stockist. Kood Circular Polariser and ND grad in sizes 84mm to 130mm cost between £25 and £35 and can be purchased from Kood direct as well as a number of camera dealers.

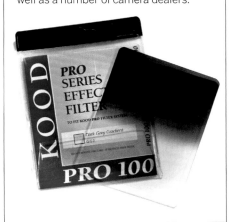

✔ Unknown brands

Search the web and you'll find filters from little-known brands like Helios. Most stem from China and as there are no official UK importers, it's hard to judge optical quality so the safest bet is to stick with recognised filter brands

Tiffen

www.tiffen.com

TIFFEN IS AN American brand that has been around for decades and is particularly popular in the movies industry. Its range of screw-in filters isn't as comprehensive as Hoya's, but it does cover all the key types including protection filters, polarisers and Neutral Density filters. It also has a number of special effect filters, in particular lots of diffusion filters including soft-focus, mist and fog, but these aren't filters you'd use on a regular basis. While the range is relatively small, quality is very high and Tiffen filters come with a ten-year guarantee. You'll also find that prices are competitive too, making them a decent alternative to brands like Hoya, although the latter is more likely to be stocked by your local photo dealer.

Choosing a tripod
Don't leave home without a three-legged friend

A TRIPOD should be viewed as an essential part of your outfit. You'll usually be using a small aperture setting to maximise depth-of-field, along with a low ISO rating to give the highest quality results, which will result in long shutter speeds. Hand-holding might be feasible with some shots but with a tripod you never need to worry about the shakes. You'll also find that by using a tripod, you can spend more time and attention on fine-tuning the framing of the scene to get the best possible composition. You'll find a huge variety of tripods on offer, so choosing one isn't straightforward, but there are two key factors to consider. The first is stability – while cheaper models may be tempting, they may not provide a stable platform. So ensure you pick a model that is sturdy enough to keep your kit totally still when shooting. The second factor to think about is how much a tripod weighs, which is important as you'll be carrying it, along with the rest of your gear, for considerable distances. Most tripods are made from aluminium, which is sturdy and fairly lightweight, although decent models weigh around 2kg or more. If you want a tripod that's as sturdy but far lighter, you'll want a carbon-fibre model, although you'll have to be prepared to pay a premium for one. Our selection of tripods have all received the highest ratings in *Digital SLR Photography* magazine. We've chosen examples that cover various price ranges to ensure you find one that suits your budget. Bear in mind that with the more expensive models, you buy the tripod and the head separately.

Interchangeable tripod heads

Most high-end tripods aren't supplied with a head. This allows users to choose their preferred legs and a specialist or general-purpose head. The two most common types of heads are as follows:

■ **Ball and socket:** These range from very simple heads with one control to complex units with panoramic locks and gauges, grip-locks, and hydraulic ball-locking systems. Usually stronger and quicker to adjust than pan and tilt heads, they allow free movement in all directions. 'Slipping' used to be a problem, not so much now, though.

■ **Three-way heads:** Commonly available as pan and tilt heads, these are good for precision work like macro photography, but are great for all types of photography. Panning gauges, showing the shooting angle, are useful for panoramic shots, although there are specialised heads made for this too. Fluid heads have the smoothest panning motion, making them ideal for sports photographers.

Ball & socket

Three-way

Features

1) HEAD There are various types of tripod head available, from ball and socket to three-way pan and tilt. Some have interchangeable heads. We have tested all the tripods here with three-way pan and tilt heads, which are the most popular for general use. When choosing a tripod, attach your camera securely and ensure the head is free from movement.

2) QUICK RELEASE PLATE These allow you to quickly attach and detach your camera to/from the tripod. All of the tripods in this review have one.

3) LEG LOCKS Most of the tripods in this test feature 'clip' locks, which are easy to use and provide a firm lock.

4) LEG SECTIONS Tripods with three leg sections or less tend to be the most sturdy, as the more sections you have, the less stable they can become.

5) SPIRIT LEVELS Useful for landscape photography in particular, many tripods feature built-in spirit levels, but if not, you your local photo store should sell one that slots on to your hotshoe.

6) BAG HOOK Some tripods have hooks on the central column, from which a bag can be hung, using its weight to add stability to the tripod in windy conditions.

7) TRIPOD FEET Spikes are good for grip outdoors but will scratch flooring. Rubber feet offer good grip indoors and outside and are the best choice for general use.

Giottos MTL9351B + MH5011 head

LENGTH (CLOSED): 64cm
NUMBER OF LEG SECTIONS: 3
HEIGHT (LEGS EXTENDED): 159cm
TYPE OF HEAD: Three-way pan and tilt
WEIGHT: 2.1kg
WEBSITE: www.giottos-tripods.com

The Giottos has very solid aluminium legs with foam insulators, to keep hands from freezing to them on cold days. The nuts and locks are a combination of plastic and die-cast aluminium, and are as solid as could be hoped for at this price. The three-way head is easily controllable and features three spirit levels in addition to the one on the legs, so there's no excuse for wonky horizons! It has a lockable rotational central column, which can be removed and re-inserted horizontally or inverted for macro or copy work. The tripod is very sturdy for the price, and comes with its own tool kit in case you need to make any adjustments. There is also a hidden bag hook underneath the central column. The MTL9351B had absolutely no problems coping with our test camera (Nikon D80) and would provide a very suitable platform on which the amateur landscaper could mount his camera outfit.

£115

Giottos Vitruvian VGR8255 kit

LENGTH (CLOSED): 40cm
HEIGHT (LEGS EXTENDED): 136cm
NUMBER OF LEG SECTIONS: 5
MAXIMUM LOAD: 4kg
WEIGHT: 1.28kg
WEBSITE: www.giottos-tripods.com

Boasting the 'reverse technology' design, the legs of the Vitruvian folds 180° to surround the centre column, reducing the length to only 40cm. Open the legs (shoulder locks provide two splay settings) and it extends to an impressive 1.36m (1.57m with centre column raised too). Made from six-layer carbon-fibre, it's lightweight and stable with aluminium alloy in the main casting adding to its robustness, while a hook on the centre column can hold ballast. Twist locks are fast and easy to use and the centre column can be removed to transform it into a monopod. The supplied MH5310-630 ball & socket head provides a smooth action and has a friction lock, spirit level and quick release plate with safety lock. The maximum load of 4kg makes this a suitable choice for most. An aluminium version (VGR 9255) has a virtually identical specification, weighs 1.5kg and costs around £180.

£250

Giottos MT8246B + MH1302-652 head

LENGTH (CLOSED): 51cm
HEIGHT (LEGS EXTENDED): 148cm
NUMBER OF LEG SECTIONS: 4
MAXIMUM LOAD: 3kg
WEIGHT: 1.375kg
WEBSITE: www.giottos-tripods.com

This tripod is exceptionally light, especially for its size, yet it is sturdy, although the maximum load may prove restrictive for some. The rubberised twist locks are secure and comfortable to use and foam leg grips give a comfortable grip in cold weather. The three-position angle locks ensure that the legs don't slip, which is reassuring to those using expensive kit. The central column is reversible for low level and macro shots, and has a bag hook. The ball and socket head is also very secure, and it is easy to manoeuvre the head into just about any position. It has a variable friction control, allowing the user a great deal of control, which means that precision adjustments are quick and easy to implement. The three spirit levels help to ensure that horizontals and verticals are perfectly aligned, making this a great all round tripod for almost any type of photography, not least landscapes.

£250

Manfrotto 190CXPRO3 + 494RC2 head

LENGTH (CLOSED): 58cm
HEIGHT (LEGS EXTENDED): 146cm
NUMBER OF LEG SECTIONS: 3
MAXIMUM LOAD: 5kg
WEIGHT: 1.62kg
WEBSITE: www.manfrotto.co.uk

This Manfrotto is exceptionally light, and its sleek design looks fantastic. Despite its thin legs, it was sturdy and supported our test camera with ease. The twist locks are very strong and prove quick to use. The central column can be raised and moved into horizontal position without removing it from the legs, making the tripod perfect for macro and low-level shots, and very easy to use. The multi-position leg locks have a depressible button, making them much easier and nicer to use than those that have clips that must be lifted. The ball and socket head is very smooth and easy to use, as one switch controls everything. This is ideal for quick positioning, but not as precise as some of the other heads in the test. There is a spirit level, to ensure that your tripod is level, and the centre column boasts a bag hook, allowing extra weight to be attached for stability in high winds.

£280

Manfrotto 190XPROB + 460MG head

LENGTH (CLOSED): 57cm
HEIGHT (LEGS EXTENDED): 146cm
NUMBER OF LEG SECTIONS: 3
MAXIMUM LOAD: 5kg
WEIGHT: 2.25kg
WEBSITE: www.manfrotto.co.uk

This aluminium tripod from Manfrotto is one of the lightest in this price category. The legs are very sturdy and supports the camera perfectly well in all positions. The flip locks are easy to open and close and very secure, and there are vari-position locks to keep the legs secure at different settings. Perhaps the most interesting feature of the legs is that the central column can be switched to horizontal position, for macro shots, without removing it from the legs. This is an excellent feature, as it makes the process very easy and fast to carry out. The head is very versatile, as it can pan, tilt and swivel in just about any direction, and is very easy to operate. The lack of panning handles may not be to everyone's taste, but the head is so versatile that it more than makes up for it. Spirit levels can be found on the head and central column brace, and a bag hook is located on the legs.

£170

Velbon Sherpa 435 With PHD-41Q head

LENGTH (CLOSED): 53cm
HEIGHT (OPEN): 161cm
NUMBER OF LEG SECTIONS: 3
WEIGHT: 1.49kg
MAX LOAD: 3kg
WEBSITE: www.intro2020.co.uk

At the more affordable end of the market is this combined head and legs set from Velbon. The tripod's black aluminium legs have three sections, locked in place with easy-to-open clip-style locks. The centre column is adjustable and reversible for low-angle shooting. For an entry-level model, the PHD-41Q head is a good buy too. It's bigger and more sturdy than others in this bracket and will take loads of up to 3kg with no problem. We like the head's relative simplicity: using it quickly becomes second nature. Two padded handles control movement, and one of these unscrews and fits inside the other when the tripod is stored. A well-designed quick-release plate completes the package. This is a cracking buy for the beginner or intermediate photographer who wants a general purpose tripod to improve their images and open more options.

£95

Manfrotto 055XPROB + 324RC2 head

LENGTH (CLOSED): 65.5cm
HEIGHT (LEGS EXTENDED): 178.5cm
NUMBER OF LEG SECTIONS: 3
MAXIMUM LOAD: 7kg
WEIGHT: 3.15kg
WEBSITE: www.manfrotto.co.uk

The build quality of this die-cast aluminium tripod is excellent. It is very sturdy, and very reassuring. The 055XPROB features the same dual positioning central column as the 190XPROB, as well as a spirit level, bag hook and foam leg grips, which help to protect the user's hands when using the tripod in cold weather. The legs each have a four-position lock, which makes it versatile and secure. You'll either love or hate the trigger-style grip head, but we found it incredibly quick and easy to adjust, getting your camera into just the right position with the minimum of fuss. Not having to tighten levers also saves time, and reduces the risk of knocking the head out of place. The head has its own spirit level, allowing you to make sure that your camera is level. This head is particularly useful when combined with the versatility of the central column and when shooting macro.

£250

Slik Pro 700DX with 700DX pan & tilt head

LENGTH (CLOSED): 76cm
HEIGHT (LEGS EXTENDED): 190cm
NUMBER OF LEG SECTIONS: 3
MAXIMUM LOAD: 6.8kg
WEIGHT: 3.2kg
WEBSITE: www.intro2020.co.uk

The largest tripod in this category is very sturdy and feels as though it could withstand any treatment. The design is simple but stylish, and it certainly looks like a tripod for serious use. Although it is quite heavy, it is still very portable for its size. The locks are strong and secure, yet easy to open, while the reversible central column allows users to take low level and macro shots with ease. This is particularly effective when used with the legs open wide, which can be done easily using the three-position locks, which hold them firmly in position. The pan-and-tilt head features a panning lock, and has a very smooth panning motion. The quick release plate is circular, which makes it very easy to attach and detach the camera. There are two spirit levels, which help to keep horizontals and verticals straight. Although there is no bag hook, the tripod is so sturdy you are unlikely to miss it.

£100

Bags and backpacks

Expert advice on storage to protect your camera gear

MOST OUTDOOR photographers prefer backpacks as they distribute weight over your shoulders and back, making it far easier to carry gear over long distances. The daypack holds photo gear in the bottom section and general items in the top compartment, while dedicated photo backpacks are designed with larger kits in mind. Consider the following:

Comfort: As you carry more kit, the weight increases, so shoulder straps are important. The wider and more padded they are, the less they dig into your shoulders. Waist straps are useful, as they relieve tension from the lumbar region and help keep your back straight. Another important factor is the bag's frame. Some are sturdier than others, this may seem uncomfortable at first, but it helps keep your back straight on long treks.

Capacity: Think about how much kit you plan to carry as this ultimately determines the size of bag you need. All the bags here have adjustable compartments so are quite versatile. We also list internal dimensions, so you can see exactly how much space they offer.

Build Quality: How well the backpack is put together, including the stitching, zippers and weatherproofing, determines how long it ought to last, how strong it is and how well it protects your equipment.

Features (see panel below): Some photographers just want a bag with lots of space, others are more demanding over specific features. Most have front pockets, designed to help you organise your memory cards and batteries into used and unused.

Fitting and wearing a bag properly

If you're carrying a lot of heavy kit, it's important that your bag sits correctly on your back or at your side. This advice can prevent all kinds of back and posture problems. With a backpack, ensure that both straps are over your shoulders and tightened so that the bag sits in the centre of your back. If it has waist and chest straps, make sure you use them to distribute the weight evenly across your back, rather than just your shoulders. For shoulder bags, pull the strap over your head to the opposite shoulder. This will distribute the weight better than if it were on the closest shoulder and stops it from slipping off your shoulder, or being easily snatched.

Gadget bag

Backpack

Features

1) STRAPS Check to see if the straps are adjustable, padded and wide, to stop them from cutting into your shoulders on long journeys. Also look for waist straps.

2) PADDING Some bags have pressure pads on the back, which will take a lot of the strain out of long journeys and spread the weight of the gear over a larger area.

3) STORAGE/CAPACITY Does the bag hold all the equipment you will need for your photography? If there is too much empty space, the bag will be unbalanced, which can be bad for your back. All the bags in this test feature adjustable dividers and offer quite a bit of versatility.

4) WEATHERPROOFING/ RAIN COVER Most bags are weather resistant. Some are weather proof, and others have all-weather covers that can be pulled out from a hidden compartment, usually on the base.

5) LAPTOP COMPARTMENT Make sure that the laptop compartment is big enough for your computer, as they vary in size. The padding is also important here.

6) ACCESSORY CLIPS Some bags allow you to attach further bags, tripods and monopods, but some are only compatible with the manufacturer's own clip systems.

7) ZIPS If you go out a lot in bad weather or near water, make sure that the zips are up to it. Wildlife photographers should also consider the noise made by the zips, as animals can be easily frightened off.

Tamrac Adventure Messenger 5

DIMENSIONS: 37x30x22cm
WEIGHT: 1.07kg
WARRANTY: Five years
CONTACT: 01628 674411
WEBSITE: www.intro2020.co.uk

If you want to carry a laptop with you, then this is a good budget choice, as it has a well-padded, laptop compartment at the rear. There is lots of internal space and comfortably holds a large DSLR, like a Nikon D700 with 24-70mm lens attached, a 70-200mm f/2.8 zoom lens and flashgun. There are four dividers to change the layout, so you could easily keep a smaller body, extra lenses, and other accessories in there too. It's not short on features either, with a padded non-slip strap, a carry handle and slots to add on components from the Tamrac Strap Accessory System. A large pocket at the front has sections for pens, stationery or note pads, a pocket in the lid for smaller items and a dedicated mobile phone pocket. If you have a medium or large DSLR, extra lenses and a laptop, this is a great buy.

BEST BUY

£50

Lowepro Classified 250 AW

DIMENSIONS (OUTER): 46.5x28x35.5cm
WEIGHT: 1.9kg
WARRANTY: Lifetime
CONTACT: 01902 864646
WEBSITE: www.lowepro.com

A discreet camera bag with room for lots of camera gear as well as a laptop. The interior of the bag is very deep, so you can double-up on storage by stacking items on top of each other. The bag's depth also makes it very suitable for cameras with long lenses. A padded section provides storage for a 15in laptop. Leather is used to good effect throughout the bag and the grab handles and shoulder strap are very well designed. Entry into the main section of the bag is through a clever roof zip that is easy to access on the move and is protected by the handle buckling over it. You'll be able to fit at least two DSLRs with an additional two or three lenses in the spacious main section. A luggage sleeve means that you can attach this bag to the handles of a wheelie case. The bag is hand-luggage friendly too.

£140

Lowepro Fastpack 250

DIMENSIONS: 31.5x24x46cm
WEIGHT: 1.6kg
WARRANTY: Lifetime
CONTACT: 01902 864646
WEBSITE: www.lowepro.com

Available in black, blue or red trim, the Fastpack 250 features two compartments and is ideal for travelling light. The camera compartment is well padded, holds a large DSLR with zoom attached, along with one or two small lenses and flash. There's no room for a second body or larger lenses though, but the rear padded pocket does hold a 15in laptop. The side entry compartment helps you get at your gear quickly, but you do need to take it off to get gear out safely. The top compartment isn't as well padded, so is not designed for camera gear, but it does include two pockets for memory cards and pens. Thanks to the generous padding on the shoulder straps and back, the Fastpack 250 is comfortable to carry, the sternum and back support straps hold it nicely in place and there's a carry handle to boot.

£65

Tamrac Aero Speed 85

DIMENSIONS: 36x23x50cm
WEIGHT: 1.6kg
WARRANTY: Five years
CONTACT: 01628 674411
WEBSITE: www.intro2020.co.uk

With space to hold personal and camera gear, the Aero Speed Pack 85 is similar to the Adventure 7, but a bit bigger, and the alternate layout allows you to carry more gear. It can hold a large DSLR, at least three lenses and it's also compatible with Tamrac's SAS system to slip on extra pouches. There's both side and front entry access, which makes getting gear out a little quicker, although you still need to take this backpack off first. The top of the bag has room for a light coat, lunch and a few other essentials, but there's no laptop compartment. Other pockets are limited too, there are a couple of side mesh pockets, and Velcro and zipped pouches for storing memory cards and batteries. Padding on the rear and non-slip straps is thin and there's no sternum strap, waist belt or rain cover either.

£90

Hama Defender 170 Pro

DIMENSIONS: 40x26x45cm
WEIGHT: 2.8kg
WARRANTY: 30 years
CONTACT: 0845 2304262
WEBSITE: www.hama.co.uk

This large backpack has two compartments, both of which feature generous space. The lower compartment fits a large DSLR with 24-70mm f/2.8 attached, a long zoom, flashgun, two small primes and even a second body. The flexible dividers make it versatile too, as the whole padded section can also be removed, and there's a large 17in laptop compartment. The construction is robust with Ultra Dobby Nylon, protected zips, tough belts, strong metal hooks and a rubber base that covers the bottom, so no problems leaving it on wet ground. The shoulder straps are adjustable, but not very well padded, and there's a waist belt, lumber support and padding on the rear for improved comfort. Features are good too, with a detachable microfibre cloth, memory card wallet, rain cover and several pockets.

£110

Lowepro Vertex 100 AW

DIMENSIONS: 30x25x42cm
WEIGHT: 2.3kg
WARRANTY: Lifetime
CONTACT: 01902 864646
WEBSITE: www.lowepro.com

This is a traditional photo backpack designed predominantly for carrying camera gear. It has water-resistant zippers, a seam-sealed All Weather finish and dedicated rain cover. The adjustable harness makes it very comfortable to carry, and there's sternum and waist support belts to help spread the load. Internal space makes it possible to squeeze in two DSLRs with lenses attached and at least three more lenses too, and there are plenty of dividers to alter the layout. There is also a 13in laptop compartment, not to mention a detachable tripod foot, and the exterior dimensions conform to the maximum hand luggage specifications for airlines too. The front pockets feature pouches for spare batteries and memory cards, there are a couple of mesh pockets for other essentials and a documents pocket, too.

£120

Lowepro Pro Runner 450 AW

DIMENSIONS: 34x29x50.5cm
WEIGHT: 2.7kg
WARRANTY: Lifetime
CONTACT: 01902 864646
WEBSITE: www.lowepro.com

The Pro Runner 450 AW holds a lot of gear, with room for two large DSLRs with zooms attached, and space for several extra lenses, flashguns, a third body and a 17in laptop too. The shoulder straps are thickly padded and adjustable, and the waist belt and carry handle will be appreciated when carting about all that weight. The compression straps help reduce the bulk on the 450AW for easier transportation, there's a built-in All Weather cover and you can carry a tripod using the loops and tripod foot. The front pocket will hold a few personal items, the three internal pockets feature windowpane panels to help keep things like filters on display, and there are two dedicated memory card pouches, too. This bag is a great option for carrying a large outfit as well as personal gear.

£135

Tamrac Expedition 7x

DIMENSIONS: 33x34x50cm
WEIGHT: 2.9kg
WARRANTY: Five years (limited)
CONTACT: 01628 674411
WEBSITE: www.intro2020.co.uk

The Expedition 7x boasts lots of room and a comfortable harness system. There's loads of padding on the shoulder straps, lumber support and waist belt, together with airflow channels to keep you cool. There's no rain cover, but water-resistant zips and a lock-down rain flap help protect your gear. The dual hinge divider system helps you carry one or two DSLRs, with zooms attached; with room to spare for other lenses, and you can boost capacity with Tamrac's Modular Accessory System and Strap Accessory System. There's a 15in laptop compartment and two 'wing' accessory pockets with Tamrac's Memory and Battery Management System for organising those essentials. There's also a plastic reinforced pocket, which provides protection for fragile accessories and acts as a tripod footrest.

£160

ADAM BURTON

Be sure to bracket!
Whether you use the grey card or not, in tricky lighting conditions, bracket your exposure by +/-1 stops using your camera's exposure compensation or AEB functions to ensure you get the shot

Metered to perfection!
Scenes with bright skies can lead to exposure error. Use a grey card and you should have no problems.

Using your free exposure metering and WB cards

The 18% grey card will ensure perfect exposures when shooting in tricky lighting conditions. Both reference cards can also be used to set a custom White Balance. Depending on your camera, you need to take a White Balance reading off the grey or the white card (your camera's instructions will show you how)

DIGITAL CAMERAS use sophisticated exposure systems and all work on the assumption that the average of the scene that is being metered from is a mid-tone, or 18% grey to be exact; i.e. the average of all dark, light and mid-tones mixed together is 18% grey. It's the basis of all metering patterns and works surprisingly well, but while it's fine for the majority of shooting situations, it can lead to incorrect exposures when the scene or subject is considerably lighter or darker in tone than 18% grey. For example, very dark areas can fool the metering system into overexposing the image. Similarly, very light subjects, such as a snow scene, can fool the camera into underexposing them as the light meter will take a reading designed to render them as a mid-tone. As a camera is trying to render an image 'grey', it's your job to ensure you compensate to keep the tones true to life. You can do this by either using one of your camera's exposure override facilities, such as exposure compensation or the AE-Lock button,

or by metering from an area of the scene that has a mid-tone. And that's where our grey card comes in. Using it is very simple as our step-by-step guide below illustrates. The key thing to remember is that you need to place the grey card in similar lighting to your scene: ie don't place it in a shaded area if your scene is bathed in sunlight. Also, make sure that the card fills the metering area – we recommend you use spot or partial metering as the card won't need to fill the entire image area – but any is suitable. You can lock the exposure using your camera's AE-Lock facility or note the aperture and shutter speed and then switch to manual mode and set these, although this method isn't suitable to days where lighting is variable. The card has AF reference lines to help your camera's autofocus lock on to it. However, you don't necessarily need it to be in focus to work correctly. The grey card (as well as the white card) can also be used to take a custom White Balance reading from, too.

1 GETTING STARTED Place your grey card on the ground angled towards you and ensure it's located in a spot that is bathed in the same light as the majority of the scene you plan to shoot.

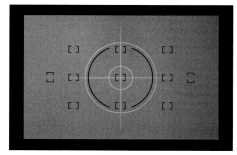

2 TAKE A METER READING Ensure that the entire metering area is filled by the grey card (in this instance we're using multi-zone metering) and lock the exposure with the AE-Lock button.

3 COMPOSE & SHOOT With this exposure locked, you can compose your scene and take your shots. When you check it on your LCD monitor, the exposure should be perfect.